HOW THE EBOOKS WORK

The eBooks are provided in EPUB file format. Please note that you will need an eBook reader installed on your device to open the file. Many devices come with this as standard, but you may still need to install one manually from Google Play.

The eBook content is identical to the content in the printed guide.

HOW TO DOWNLOAD
THE WALKING EYE APP

1. Download the Walking Eye App from the App Store or Google Play.
2. Open the app and select the scanning function from the main menu.
3. Scan the QR code on this page – you will then be asked a security question to verify ownership of the book.
4. Once this has been verified, you will see your eBook in the purchased ebook section, where you will be able to download it.

Other destination apps and eBooks are available for purchase separately or are free with the purchase of the Insight Guide book.

Contents

Jersey's Top 10 6

Queen of the Channel 8

Food and Drink 12

Walks and Tours

1 **St Helier** 14

Liberation Square 15, Maritime Museum and Tapestry Gallery 16, Church of St Helier 18, Streets and Sewers 19, Royal Square 20, Central Market 22, Fish Market 23, Jersey Museum and Art Gallery 24, Elizabeth Castle 25, The Waterfront 29

Feature: War Tunnels 32

2 **The Southwest** 34

St Aubin's Bay 34, St Aubin 36, Noirmont Point 39, Portelet Bay 39, Ouaisné Bay 40, St Brelade's Bay 41

3 **The West Coast** 46

La Corbière 46, St Ouen's Bay 48

Feature: Fables and Festivals 56

4 **Flowers and Farming** 58

Battle of Flowers 59, Waterworks Valley 60, Hamptonne Country Life Museum 60, Tamba Park 62, La Mare Wine Estate 62, St Peter's Valley 63, Jersey Lavender 64, Detour to Eric Young Orchid Foundation 66

5 The North Coast **68**

Rozel 69, Bouley Bay 69, Bonne Nuit 71, La Crête Fort 73, Devil's Hole 74, Grève de Lecq 75, Plémont 76, Les Landes 77, Grosnez Castle 78, North Coast Footpath 80

Feature: Hall of Fame **82**

6 Sights of the East **84**

La Hougue Bie 85, Mont Orgueil Castle 88, Gorey Harbour 91, St Catherine's Bay 92, Royal Bay of Grouville 93, Seymour Tower 94, Green Island 95, Ramsar Site 96, Botanic Gardens at Samarès Manor 96, Le Dicq and Victor Hugo 98

7 Durrell's Wildlife **100**

Durrell's Legacy 101, The Perfect Setting 102, Saved from the Brink 103, Gentle Jambo 104

Travel Tips

Active Pursuits **108**

Themed Holidays **114**

Practical Information **115**

Accommodation **122**

Index **127**

Jersey's Top 10

Spectacular cliff paths, stunning coastal scenery, beautiful gardens, historic forts and castles, and museums chronicling the island's rich heritage – here at a glance are the high spots of Jersey

▲ **Jersey War Tunnels.** The dark, dank tunnels and evocative displays are a harrowing reminder of Jersey under the Germans. See page 32.

▲ **Elizabeth Castle.** Take the Castle Ferry to see this Tudor fort, which defended the island for over 300 years. See page 25.

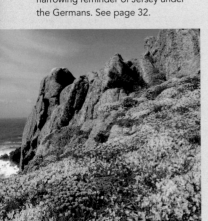

▲ **North Coast Footpath.** Flower-clad cliff paths extend all along the northern coast, offering bracing walks and stunning views. See page 80.

▶ **Maritime Museum.** Explore the island's links with the sea and its former role as a seafaring state. See page 16.

▼ **Surfing.** Ride the big Atlantic swell which pounds the 4-mile (6km) sandy bay of St Ouen's – or just sit and watch the surfing pros. See page 49.

▲ **Mont Orgueil Castle.** Climb the ramparts of this medieval fortress for splendid views of the east coast and Normandy, across the water. See page 88.

▼ **La Hougue Bie.** A huge mound conceals one of the largest and best-preserved Neolithic passage graves in Europe. See page 85.

▲ **Samarès Manor.** This fine manor is a horticultural haven with acres of landscaped gardens, a plant nursery and spectacular herb garden. See page 96

▼ **Jersey Zoo.** No ordinary zoo, Durrell has been saving species on the brink for more than 60 years. See page 100.

▲ **Jersey Museum and Art Gallery.** Steep yourself in Jersey's history at this award-winning museum. See page 24.

Catching some rays on St Brelade's beach.

Overview

Queen of the Channel

A tiny island in the shadow of France, Jersey packs in big beaches, stunning seascapes and a host of historic and family attractions

When the novelist Victor Hugo was exiled from France he chose to live on the island closest to home — just 14 miles (22km) across the Channel, where his native language was spoken. "Fragments of Eu-

rope dropped by France and picked up by England", was how he described the Channel Islands. As self-governing islands and strongholds of ancient, semi-feudal laws, the Channel Islands are neither truly British, nor are they French. English is now the accepted language, the currency is pounds and pence, yet many street names are still in French, the food has a Gallic slant and the islands have a distinctly foreign flavour. Tourists are drawn by this combination of French flavour and British lifestyle — not to mention the location, which is sufficiently far south to guarantee more daily hours of sun than anywhere else in Britain.

For a small island Jersey offers a wide range of attractions and activities, from ancient castles and war-

time relics to sea sports and cycle tours, spas and adventure parks. But for most visitors it's the coastline that has the greatest allure. Jersey has 50 miles (80km) of shoreline and 20 miles (32km) of fine sandy beaches, swept clean by huge tides. The island tilts southwards, and seascapes range from the towering cliffs of the north to the Atlantic rollers of the west and the spacious sands of the south. The island has one of the largest tidal movements in the world, and the coastal landscape undergoes dramatic changes between high and low water.

LOCATION AND CLIMATE

The most southerly of the British Isles, Jersey lies in the Gulf of St Malo, 100 miles (160km) from mainland Britain, but only 14 miles (22km) from the coast of Normandy. On most days you can see France from the north and east coasts. Largest of the Channel Islands, Jersey is 9 miles (14km) east to west, 5 miles (8km) north to south. In summer the island has a daily average

The Jersey cow pops up everywhere on the island.

Toads and Donkeys

Deep-rooted rivalries exist between Jersey and Guernsey. To Guernsey natives Jersey is "the other island" and the inhabitants are *crapauds* (toads), while Jersey people refer to the residents of their supposedly stubborn little sister as *ânes* (donkeys).

The *crapaud*, which is found only on Jersey, has been fast disappearing from ponds and waterways. The Durrell Wildlife Conservation Trust, renowned for recovering endangered species from more exotic climes, is currently helping to save the island mascot.

of eight hours of sunshine and an average maximum temperature of 68°F (20°C). As in the UK, there is always the risk of bad weather, but clouds are often quickly dispersed by the strong south-westerly winds.

BRITISH LINKS

The Channel Islands once formed part of the Duchy of Normandy but have had links with the British Isles ever since the Battle of Hastings, when they became part of the Anglo-Norman realm. The links were reinforced in 1204 when King John lost

Jersey Royals are one of the most prized crops of spring.

Normandy to France but the Channel Islands chose to remain loyal to the English crown. In return for their allegiance King John granted the islands customs and privileges, tantamount to self-government, which have since been confirmed by every English monarch. France then became the enemy, and for the next 650 years Jersey was repeatedly threatened by French invasions. The last invaders were the Nazi Germans, who occupied the Channel Islands in World War II.

LANGUAGE

Until the 1960s French was still the official language of Jersey. Prayers are still said in French before States and court sittings, and the parliament votes *pour* or *contre*. Not so long ago a Jersey resident would have spoken English, standard French and Jèrriais, a derivation of ancient Jersey-Norman. This *patois* enjoyed a revival during the German Occupation as a useful means of covert communication, and today it can very occasionally be heard by elderly Jersiais (the people who speak it). Only a handful of the population speak it fluently, but renewed interest in the language has led to the introduction of classes in some schools.

The English language was first introduced to Jersey in the 18th century, and is now spoken by all the islanders. Street names on the island still carry their French names, often very different from the English names they were later given, eg La Rue de Derrière (King Street) or La Rue des Trois Pigeons (Hill Street).

ECONOMY

The all-dominant financial services industry accounts for over 40 percent of the total economic activity on Jersey, employing around a fifth of the workforce. This took over from ag-

Anne Port, a pleasant cove on the northeast of the island, is an ideal location for rockpooling with children.

riculture and tourism as the mainstay of the economy in the latter part of the 20th century. Tourism generates less than 4 percent of Jersey's GVA though the total impact of the sector is equivalent to 8.3 percent of GVA. The decade-long downward trend in travel to Jersey was reversed in 2017 when the island saw 727,000 visits, putting it on track to achieve its aim of one million visitors by 2030.

Since Napoleonic times Jersey has attracted high-earning immigrants seeking to benefit from the island's desirable way of life and advantageous tax laws. Today's high earners are actively encouraged through the High Value Residency initiative, whereby applications are assessed for suitability on social and economic grounds, including paying a minimum tax of tax of £145,000 per annum.

ENVIRONMENT

To date Jersey has 19 Sites of Special Interest (SSIs), protected for ecological and geological interest, plus a huge intertidal zone designated as a Ramsar site (a wetland of international importance) on the southeast coast. The island's 16 beaches are washed by some of the cleanest waters in Europe.

Green lanes, reducing the speed limit on some country lanes to 15mph (24kmh), have encouraged cyclists and pedestrians, and clearly marked cycle routes now cover 96 miles (155km) of coast and countryside. On the negative side, although the island is still largely unspoilt its capital, St Helier has seen very unsightly development swallowing up the coastline. The amount of rubbish generated has doubled in 20 years and the island only recycles a third of its waste. Jersey still has one of the highest car ownership and user rates in the world. It's remarkable how many Porsches and other fast cars you see given that the maximum speed limit on the island is 40mph (64kmh)!

Guide to Coloured Boxes

Eating	This guide is dotted with coloured boxes providing additional practical and cultural information to make the most of your visit. Here is a guide to the coding system.
Fact	
Green	
Kids	
Shopping	
View	

Food and Drink

Jersey has a thriving gastronomic scene and the islanders are spoilt for choice. Within its 45-mile (70km) radius there are around 200 restaurants including four with Michelin stars. A vast array of fabulously fresh seafood and fish is caught around the shores, and that's not the only local produce. Jersey produces its own vegetables, fruit, herbs, beef, pork and even cheeses. Not to mention the famous Jersey Royal potatoes and the rich creamy milk from Jersey cows.

For the islanders fishing has always been a way of life. In the Middle Ages the abundance of conger eel, which was salted, dried and shipped to England, led to the nickname "Isle of the Congers". From the 16th century fortunes were made from the cod banks of Newfoundland. Conger numbers have declined, but lobsters, scallops, crabs, bass, mackerel and grey mullet are still fished from Jersey shores, and around 4 million

A hearty bowl of traditional Jersey bean crock.

oysters are farmed annually at the Royal Bay of Grouville.

The island works hard to promote its food with an annual food festival and the six-week Tennerfest in October-November when

The Jersey Ormer

The indigenous ormer, related to the abalone, is now so rare that fishing is only permitted between October and April on the first day of each new or full moon, and the five days following. Ormers cooked in a casserole with belly of pork, shallots and carrot used to be a daily dish, the mother-of-pearl shell used as an ashtray or thrown away.

Occasionally you'll see locals scouring the rocks for the prized molluscs, but long gone are the days when they featured on restaurant menus.

The iridescent ear-shaped shell of the ormer.

over 100 restaurants offer fixed-price menus from £10. Prosperous resident financiers and lawyers keep the upmarket restaurants in business, and even the discerning French come across the Channel to indulge their palates. St Helier boasts the highly rated Bohemia and Ormer(see page 31); St Aubin, St Brelade and Gorey all have an excellent choice, from smart seafood restaurants to beachside cafés serving home-made cakes and Jersey cream teas. Even in tiny Rozel, right up in the north, you can choose between a legendary crab sandwich at the Hungry Man kiosk, hand-dived scallops at The Rozel or a succulent T-bone steak at Château La Chaire.

ISLAND SPECIALITIES

A few island favourites survive from bygone days. The misleadingly named **black butter**(du nièr beurre) is an apple preserve that used to be made in vast quantities every autumn. Typical recipes comprised 700lb of apples, 10 gallons of cider, 20lb of sugar, 24 lemons and 3lb of spices. Cooking carried on all day and night, with family members stirring the huge pot and making merry with song and dance. La Mare Vineyards (see page 62) make their own black butter and sell it at their estate and at St Helier market.

Just occasionally you come across **Jersey bean crock**, a variation of the French cassoulet, comprising five different kinds of dried beans, pig's trotter, belly of pork or shin of beef, carrot and onion. The hearty dish is served with cabbage loaf, a crusty white bread baked in large cabbage leaves. At festivals and other island events look out for les Mèrvelles or Jersey Wonders, doughnut-like cakes in the shape of an 8 – traditionally cooked as the tide goes out.

JERSEY FIZZ

Cider used to be the island tipple, and large quantities were exported from the mid-17th century to the mid-19th century. One of the few places where cider is made today is La Mare Wine Estate, which produces a sparkling form, similar to the Normandy cidre bouché. La Mare is on the same latitude as Champagne and produces the very palatable sparkling white Le Mourier, using the méthode traditionelle and a pink sparkler called Lillie, after Jersey-born Lillie Langtry.

Find our recommended restaurants at the end of each Tour. Below is a Price Guide to help you make your choice.

Jersey cows provide many tasty local treats.

The stunning setting of Elizabeth Castle.

Tour 1

St Helier

This walk around Jersey's capital, visiting two of the best museums, the lively Central Market and historic Elizabeth Castle, is 2½ miles (4km) and takes a whole day

Jersey's capital is home to two of the best museums on the island, a spectacularly located historic castle and a central square steeped in history. Although the traffic in the capital is worse than anywhere else on the island, the main shopping thoroughfares, with large stores, boutiques and lively food markets, are pedestrianised. The walk takes you through the historic centre, west to Elizabeth Castle and back along the waterfront.

The town's origins date back to the 6th century when Helerius, a monk from modern-day Belgium, founded a hermitage on a small rocky outcrop on a tidal islet in St Aubin's Bay, today known as the Hermitage Rock. Helerius devoted his life to prayer and

Highlights

- Maritime Museum and Occupation Tapestry Gallery
- Royal Square
- Central Market and Fish Market
- Jersey Museum and Art Gallery
- Elizabeth Castle

fasting, but in AD 555, after 15 years on the island, he was beheaded by a band of passing pirates. A small monastic settlement rose up here, and in the 12th century, an oratory was dedicated to St Helier.

Growth over the centuries was slow and it was not until entrepreneurial Huguenot refugees arrived in the 16th and 17th centuries,

Hermitage Rock.

land was reclaimed from the sea, and by 1840 St Helier had taken over from St Aubin as the island's main harbour.

LIBERATION SQUARE

Start at **Liberation Square ❶**, which was opened by Prince Charles on 9 May 1995, the 50th anniversary of the Liberation of the island from German Occupation. It was here that jubilant crowds greeted the British liberators after five long years under German rule. To mark the 70th anniversary of Liberation in May 2015, Jersey and the other Channel Islands celebrated with a host of entertainment and activities, stretching over five weeks.

bringing their skills with them, that the town saw any real expansion. Further growth came about in the late 18th century, funded by all the profits from privateering during the French and American wars. In the post-Napoleonic era, the population was swelled when hundreds of officers from the English army settled in the town. Retired on half pay, they were lured to Jersey by the climate, the low cost of living and the desirable lifestyle. Regency and Victorian houses were constructed,

The prominent **Liberation Sculpture** commemorates the event with a bronze group of figures, holding up the Union flag. From left to right the figures represent a Jersey couple old enough to have witnessed the Occupation, a liberator, a Jersey fisherman and a farmer with his wife and children. Overlooking the square on the north side, the Pomme d'Or Hotel was the headquarters of the German navy during the Occupation.

The square used to be the terminus of the Jersey Railway which served the

The bronze Liberation Sculpture in Liberation Square.

The Maritime Museum on New North Quay.

south and east coasts, and it was from the rear of the building on the west side that some 2,200 residents were deported to Germany in September 1942.

Alongside Liberation Square is Liberty Wharf, a covered shopping mall of independent boutiques and major brand stores within original granite warehouses.

MARITIME MUSEUM AND TAPESTRY GALLERY

Across the busy A1 south of Liberation Square, and looking like some-

16 New Street

The early Georgian House at 16 New Street, west of Central Market, has been restored to its former elegance. Originally the home of a public notary, it has served as the HQ of the Liberty Gentlemen's Club and latterly the workshop of de Gruchy, the Jersey department store. By the 1980s it was neglected and demolition was threatened. However the National Trust bought the property for £1 in 2003 and thanks to a £1 million bequest by the late Mollie Houston, who moved to Jersey after WWII, the Trust was able to undertake a meticulous renovation.

thing out of Disneyland, the world's largest **Steam Clock** is modelled on a 19th-century paddle steamer. Local vessels and shipbuilders are commemorated on benches around the harbour.

The nearby **Maritime Museum ❷** (www.jerseyheritage.org; Apr–Oct daily 10am–5pm, Nov– mid Dec and Jan-Mar Sun only, 10am–4pm), housed in a restored warehouse on **New North Quay**, explores every aspect of the island's links with the sea. Jersey was one of the largest shipbuilding centres in Europe, its shipyards around the coast producing over 800 wooden sailing ships in the mid-19th century. From

the 1860s the trade suffered from the advent of iron and steam.

This first-rate museum offers a host of hands-on exhibits and other activities for visitors of all ages. You can feel the pull of the currents and the power of the sea, design a boat and listen to songs and salty tales of the past. Among the highlights are a full-size replica of the bow of the Jersey-built brig, the *Orient Star*, and the 'Voyages Globe', a giant animatronic globe illustrating the journeys of Jersey's ships all over the world. On Mondays, Tuesdays and Wednesdays you can watch the declining art of boat-building as volunteers repair and maintain

Salty sea dogs in the Maritime Museum.

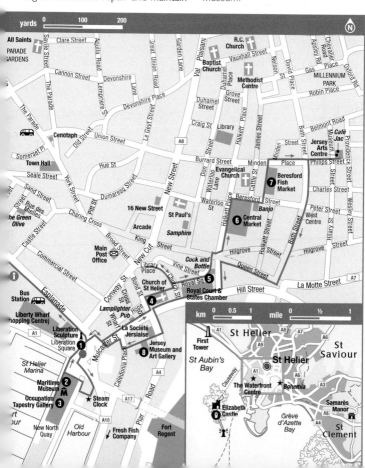

There are 12 richly embroidered tapestries in the Occupation Tapestry Gallery, detailing the moving story of life in Jersey during World War II.

the museum's fleet of historic vessels. Examples of the restored boats can sometimes be seen in the marina outside the museum.

Occupation Tapestry Gallery

Within the museum is the **Occupation Tapestry Gallery** ❸ comprising 12 separate large tapestries charting the story of the Occupation from the arrival of the Germans to their surrender to the British liberators in 1945.

These historically accurate and meticulously worked scenes were created by the 12 Jersey parishes to commemorate the 50th anniversary of Liberation. Themes range from 'The Outbreak of War' and 'Deportation' to 'The Daily Life of Civilians', such as the school-room scene of a boy yawning in a German lesson.

Return to Liberation Square, cross the Esplanade on the far side and take Mulcaster Street. About halfway up the road you'll see the **Lamplighter Pub**, decorated with stuccowork depicting the figure of Britannia between two cherubs and a garland of fruit below. This was the work of Turnkey Giffard, a prison warden who enter-

tained his inmates by showing them how to carve. Take the next turning left into **Bond Street**, where Regency and Victorian buildings retain some of their original features.

CHURCH OF ST HELIER

On the right stands the pink granite **Church of St Helier** ❹ (normally open during daylight hours), the largest of the parish churches. The seafront used to come right up to the church,

Looking up to the square tower of the Church of St Helier.

and the square tower served as a useful observation post. The stretch of land between here and the sea was reclaimed from the end of the 18th century for town housing and warehouses.

The gate at the far end of the railings formed part of a screen used to segregate male and female prisoners during services in the Debtors' Prison. Major Peirson, hero of the Battle of Jersey (see page 21), is buried in the centre of the church, while Baron de Rullecourt, who led the enemy, merely has a simple memorial in the churchyard; the location of his grave is unknown.

STREETS AND SEWERS

Leave the church by the north side for **Church Street**. The name of the street looks somewhat prosaic beside the former French name, **La Rue Trousse Cotillon** or Pick Up Your Petticoat Street. The name dates from a less salubrious era when ladies had to lift up their dresses to avoid the drains and sewers. English settlers in St Helier in the mid-19th century replaced some of the French street names with English alternatives that had no connection at all with the originals.

It was in the house on the opposite side of the road (now the United Club) where John Wesley, founder of Methodism, preached the Gospel in 1787. Wesley, who visited Jersey, Guernsey and Alderney, had a profound influence on the islanders, and by the 1820s chapels, large and small, in the vernacular Gothic or classical styles, were appearing all over the islands. The **St Helier Methodist Centre** (formerly the Wesley Grove Methodist Church) at the top

St Helier

The hermit Helerius was murdered by axe-wielding Saxon pirates. He was later canonised, and his death is commemorated by the pair of crossed axes which feature on the St Helier parish crest. According to local folklore, after Helerius was murdered, he picked up his severed head and carried it for 200 metres/yds to the shore. Every year on the Sunday closest to 16 July, St Helier's day, a procession makes its way to the Hermitage Rock and a wreath is laid at the entrance of the oratory which was built over his cave.

Annual pilgrimage to Hermitage Rock.

Bullet holes, fired by troops in the 1781 Battle of Jersey, can still be seen in the walls of the Peirson Pub in the now peaceful Royal Square.

of Halkett Place used to seat 1,600. Methodism still has a strong influence on many of the islanders and several of the churches are still in use.

Further along on the corner is **Jersey's first library**, a Georgian building and one of the first on the island to be made of brick. At the end of Library Place, to the left, the **obelisk** was erected in 1855 to Pierre le Sueur, the Constable of St Helier who transformed the town by ridding the streets of streams of sewage, providing clean water, and installing a complete underground system.

ROYAL SQUARE

Retrace your steps to Church Street, turning left into **Royal Square ❺**, formerly the Market Place, where weekly markets-cum-fairs took place, prisoners awaited trial in a cage (public executions took place nearby) and where, on occasions, witches were burnt. Devil worship had spread to Jersey by the late 16th century, and witch trials were common. The sentence for a convicted witch was 'to be hanged and strangled by the public executioner till death en-

sues, after that her body to be burned and entirely consumed'.

The name Market Place was changed to Royal Square in honour of King George II (1727–60), who donated £200 towards the creation of St Helier's first harbour. An ostentatious statue of the king in the square shows him dressed as Caesar. Below the statue a proclamation stone commemorates the day in February 1649 when Jersey proclaimed Charles II King of England, after the execution of his father. During the English Civil War, the island had

The gilded statue of George II, posing as Caesar, in Royal Square.

Attractive 17th-century houses are now home to jewellers' shops.

This was the last attempt by France to capture the island. The young hero was immortalised in John Singleton Copley's painting of *The Death of Major Peirson* at London Tate Britain Gallery, a copy of which hangs in the Royal Court on Royal Square.

Royal Square today

Today Royal Square is a peaceful, shady spot, providing a retreat from the town traffic and alfresco pubs and cafés where. you can sit with a drink and watch the world go by. The building nearest to Church Street is the former **Corn Market**, preserving the original granite arches inside and now home to the Registry Office.

If you look carefully at the paving stones on this side of the square you'll see a carved 'V' for Victory. This was cut by a local stonemason while relaying the stones during the German Occupation. Discovery could have led to deportation, so he hid the 'V' under a layer of sand. The letters 'EGA' and '1945' were added after the Swedish Red Cross ship, the SS *Vega*, arrived towards the end of the Occupation with 750 tons of food parcels, relieving the islanders from near-starvation.

provided Charles with refuge on two occasions, the first time as the young Prince of Wales. He was not crowned king in England until 1660, and for over 10 years he was acknowledged as the rightful king only in Jersey and Scotland. As a reward for Jersey's loyalty, Charles gave Smith's Island and some neighbouring islets off Virginia to Sir George Carteret with permission to settle. Carteret renamed them New Jersey.

Battle of Jersey

In the centre of Royal Square a stone commemorates the Battle of Jersey, which took place in 1781. A French force of 600, led by Baron de Rullecourt, secretly landed at night on the southeastern tip of the island, at La Rocque. The Lieutenant-Governor of Jersey, Moses Corbet, who was still in bed, surrendered, tricked into believing that the French had an overwhelming army. But the British soldiers and Jersey Militia refused to lay down their arms and a heroic young English officer, Major Francis Peirson, led the local troops to victory in a brief but bloody battle in Royal Square. Both de Rullecourt and Peirson were killed in action.

Jersey's Constitution

The constitution of the States of Jersey comprises the offices of Bailiff, Lieutenant-Governor, who is the monarch's representative on the island, the Dean of Jersey, the Attorney General and the Solicitor General – along with 8 senators, 12 parish constables and 29 deputies who are all democratically elected. The old committee system was abolished in 2005 and ministerial government introduced. A number of scrutiny panels keep an eye on the policies of the executive.

The Royal Court

On the south side of Royal Square, the central building is the **Royal Court** (1866), the island's court of justice, with the arms of George II above the entrance. It was from the balcony to the right that Alexander Coutanche, Bailiff of Jersey, hoisted the Union flag on 8 May 1945 and relayed to the huge crowds Churchill's message that the Channel Islands were to be liberated. East of here is the **States Chamber**, the island's parliament.

CENTRAL MARKET

Peirson Place, beside the pub, leads to King Street (formerly Rue Derrière), a busy pedestrianised shopping thoroughfare. Turn right along King Street for Halkett Place, named after a former Lieutenant-Governor of Jersey who served with distinction at the Battle of Waterloo. Cross the street and turn left for the **Central Market** ❻ (Mon–Sat 7.30am–5.30pm,

Thu until 2.30pm). Market stalls were banned from Royal Square in 1800 and a new site chosen on the corner of Halkett Place and Beresford Street.

The original was a splendid grand building, modelled on the City of Bath market. But to celebrate the centenary of the Battle of Jersey a new market was constructed in 1881 – which is the one you see today. This is a fine glass-roofed building with a wonderful array of fresh produce, including strawberries, asparagus, Jersey herbs and home-grown flowers. Apart from fruit and veg there are butchers and bakers, cafés, restaurants and delis selling island specialities.

Outside the post office in the Central Market, the red hexagonal pillar box (1851) designed by the novelist Anthony Trollope, was, according to Jersey, the very first in the British Isles. They were originally painted green, and it wasn't until 1874 that the post boxes were painted the familiar red.

Watch out for giant lobsters at the Fish Market.

The Central Market entrance.

Market Shopping

Central Market overflows with culinary delights special to Jersey. Look out for *les Mèrvelles* (small doughnuts), *du nièr beurre* (apple preserve), and cabbage loaf (bread baked wrapped in cabbage leaves).

FISH MARKET

Leave the Central Market at the Beresford Street exit and turn right. Across the road, the **Fish Market** ❼ (also known as Beresford Market) has a spectacular selection of seafood and fish, both local and imported. Head down here at 7.30am to see the arrival of the catch of the day or make it later and enjoy a seafood lunch and glass of wine at The Blue Ocean within the market. From the Jersey waters come sea bass, wrasse, grey mullet, shrimps, live lobsters, spider and chancre crabs, bream and

Fresh market produce.

mackerel. Look out too for conger eels, though long gone are the days when these were caught in profusion around the Jersey shores. In the 17th century congers were so popular and abundant that the Channel Islands acquired the nickname of 'the Kingdom of Congers'.

Exit the Fish Market at its northern end, turn right along Minden Place and cross over Bath Street for the **Jersey Arts Centre** (www.artscentre.je), a short way along on the left. This provides a broad range of the performing and visual arts for all ages and has an excellent café serving food all day (see page 31). Return to Bath Street, turning left for the West Centre, where you'll meet a family of bronze Jersey cows, and a tiny toad or *crapaud*.

At the end of Bath Street, turn right into **Queen Street**, which with King Street, is the town's main shopping thoroughfare. The next left will bring you into Hill Street, the street of advocates bristling with brass nameplates. Turn right for Mulcaster Street and first left for Pier Road.

Just up the hill on the right is **La Société Jersiaise** (www.societe-jersiaise.org), founded in 1873 and dedicated to the study of the history, archaeology and natural history of the island, the conservation of the environment and historic buildings, and the establishment of an Island museum.

JERSEY MUSEUM AND ART GALLERY

Occupying a townhouse which used to stand on the seafront, the award-winning **Jersey Museum and Art Gallery** ❽ (www.jerseyheritage.org; late Mar–Oct Mon-Sat 8.30am–5pm, Sun 10am–5pm, Nov–Dec Mon-Sat 9am–4pm, Sun 10am–4pm. Jan–Feb Mon-Sat 9am–5pm, Sun 10am–4pm,) gives you an excellent insight into Jersey life and history over the ages.

The house was built in 1818 by a wealthy shipowner who contributed in 1820 to the cost of land reclamation and a harbour-building scheme (now Commercial Buildings). The two upper floors have been lovingly restored and fitted out with period furniture to show how it would have looked like in Victorian times, when it was occupied by a doctor and his family.

The exhibition starts with a re-creation of the Old Stone Age site of La Cotte de St Brelade, showing the figures of Palaeolithic man on the rock face and the bones of prehistoric woolly rhino found at the foot of the cave. The finds at

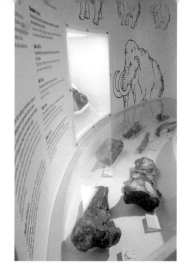

Ancient remains on display at the Jersey Museum.

this Old Stone Age site prove that primitive man used the ravine as a 'funnel trap', charging the prehistoric beasts over the cliff edge to their deaths. On the same floor, don't miss the Story of Jersey film, with fascinating pre-war footage of Jersey; nor Lillie Langtry's immaculate Victorian travelling case.

Elizabeth Castle from Hermitage Rock.

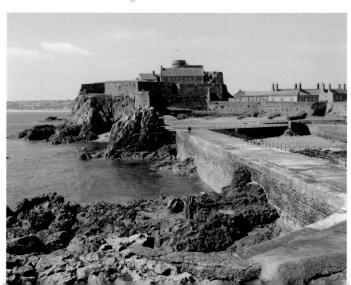

The Jersey Lily

Highlights of Jersey Museum's art gallery are the two portraits of Lillie Langtry, by John Everett Millais and Sir Edward Poynter. Renowned for her beauty and pure white skin, she was nicknamed the Jersey Lily (the flower she is holding in Millais's painting is in fact a Guernsey not a Jersey lily). Both portraits caused a sensation at London's Royal Academy in 1878 – when Lillie was the acknowledged mistress of the Prince of Wales.

When Jersey's cave dwellers were stampeding rhino and mammoth off the clifftops Jersey was still attached to the Continent. A display on the first floor shows how the sea level rose and the Channel Islands were formed. A spectacular long torc in twisted gold, discovered in St Helier, hints at the prosperity of the Bronze Age, pre-2000 BC. Other exhibits cover the main events of the island's dramatic history as well as traditions and trades such as shipbuilding, knitting and oyster catching.

ELIZABETH CASTLE

No visit to St Helier is really complete without a trip to **Elizabeth Castle** ❾ one of Jersey's major historic monuments (www.jerseyheritage.org; Easter–Oct daily 10am–5.30pm, last admission 5pm). Lying on an islet in St Aubin's Bay, the castle can be reached via the Esplanade, beyond Liberation Square, on the landward side. Follow signs for the tourist office, then continue on the Esplanade until you see the Castle Ferry kiosk on the waterfront. Visitors can either go by foot along the 0.6-mile (1km) causeway at low tide or catch the amphibious Castle Ferry (not included in the castle entrance fee), which travels at all tides.

Construction on the castle began in the late 16th century, by which time Mont Orgueil (see page 89), built for bows and arrows, was becoming increasingly exposed. Sir Walter Raleigh, the island's Governor, who lived at the castle from 1600, called it Fort Isabella Bellissima (Elizabeth the most Beautiful), in tribute to his Queen, Elizabeth I. It was not until the 1640s, when Jersey had been drawn into the English Civil War, that the castle – which by now had grown considerably in size – came into its own. Charles II, then Prince of Wales, took refuge

The Jersey Museum, a superb four-storey merchant's house.

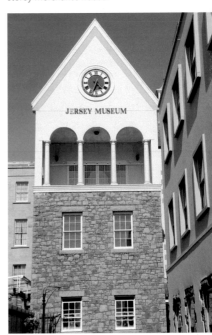

Elizabeth Castle is accessible at all times by the amphibious Castle Ferry, or on foot at low tide.

here, and did so again after the execution of his father. During the war, Sir Philip Carteret, then Governor, resisted a siege here for 50 days, and the castle was the last of Jersey's strongholds to surrender. Defeat came in December 1651 when a shell from St Helier Hill (now Fort Regent) hit the abbey church and exploded the powder magazine.

Fit for a King

Follow in the footsteps of Sir Walter Raleigh and King Charles II and stay at Jersey's famous fortress. The small apartment (sleeping 4–6) within Elizabeth Castle may not be on the same scale as the Governor's house in the 17th century, but for those with a sense of adventure it's a wonderful spot to stay. Tides isolate the castle twice daily, but amphibious ferries provide a service during opening hours (bookings through Jersey Heritage at www.jerseyheritage.org).

The Parliamentarians held Jersey for the next nine years.

Visiting the Castle

The fortifications you see today are divided into three: the oldest, **Upper Ward**, at the top, the **Lower Ward** beneath it and finally the **Outer Ward**. The oldest sections date from the 17th century, with the Guard House, hospital and workshops added in the early 19th century. The buildings around the **Parade Ground** house exhibitions covering the history of the castle, the development of the cannon and the story of the Royal Jersey Militia. The Militia served the island for around 600 years, and in their heyday numbered over 6,000 local men, divided into five regiments. To reinforce the military theme, Gunner Graves fires the noonday gun.

From the Parade Ground it's easy to miss the access up to the older Upper Ward, also called the Mount. For the best views of the coast, climb up to the gunnery control tower. This was built by the Ger-

Join in the re-enactment of the Gunner's Parade at Elizabeth Castle.

mans, who modernised the castle with bunkers and battlements. Over to the east you can see Fort Regent, which took over as the island's main fortress after Elizabeth Castle. Built into the mount is the Governor's

Aerial view of cottages on Les Minquiers.

house, where Sir Walter Raleigh lived – though he was off the island for most of his tenure.

On regular days throughout the season history is kept alive at the castle by displays of artillery, military parades and firing of the black powder cannons. There is plenty of audience participation, and visitors may be dragooned into drill practice and marching the Parade Ground!

Views to Fort Regent

Fort Regent, visible from Elizabeth Castle, was built in 1806–14 on a granite hill above St Helier and took over as the island's main fortress. It was built at enormous expense as a protection against further attacks from France. Napoleon had acted angrily over Jersey profiteering from French vessels: 'France can tolerate no longer this nest of brigands and assassins. Europe must be purged of this vermin. Jersey is England's shame.' Troops were stationed

Les Minquiers

From Elizabeth Castle's gunnery control tower views stretch all the way south to Les Minquiers (known as 'The Minkies'), a group of rocky islets 9 miles (14km) offshore. Ownership of the reef and that of Les Ecréhous, the rocky islets between Jersey and Normandy, has on occasions been a matter of dispute between Jersey (backed by the UK) and France. In 1953 a battle was fought out at the International Court of Justice in The Hague. England won, much to the chagrin of the French. There are still occasional attempts to raise the Tricolore on the reefs, mainly by French fishermen asserting a claim to fishing rights off the islets.

General Conway's Dolmen

In 1785, during defence constructions on the hill where Fort Regent now stands, an extensive dolmen was discovered resembling a mini Stonehenge. Since the grave was impeding construction of the fort, it was presented as a retirement present to General Conway, then Governor of the island. The capstones and mighty megaliths – each weighing around 140 tons – were shipped across the Channel and taken up the Thames to grace the general's private estate upstream from Henley-on-Thames, where the dolmen stands today.

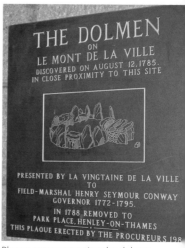

Plaque commemorating the dolmen, Vingtaine de la Ville.

here for many years, but the French threat ended with the English victories at Trafalgar in 1805 and Waterloo in 1815, and the fort was never actually to fulfil its function. Today the most conspicuous feature of the fort is the modern white dome above the walls and bastions which survive from the original structure.

In 1958 the fort was sold back to the States of Jersey for £14,500, the original price of the land, and the building was then converted into a leisure centre.

The fort used to be the site of the last working signal station in the British Isles, used for weather warnings, high tides, shipping movements – and

La Frégate café, resembling an upturned boat, is part of St Helier's Waterfront.

Freedom Tree sculpture by Richard Perry, on the Waterfront.

The Union flag on the west bastion is lowered to half-mast only when a monarch dies, though an exception was made on the death of Diana, Princess of Wales.

THE WATERFRONT

As you leave Elizabeth Castle – whether by foot or amphibious craft – the views to the west are rather more alluring than those to the east.

Indeed, St Helier's **Waterfront** ❿ is Jersey's eyesore, characterised by a series of utilitarian high-rise buildings and large car parks. At drawing-board stage the aim was to 'breathe new life into the town and the island, enriching the quality of life for resident and visitor alike'. The leisure centre, clubs and fast-food outlets attract some of Jersey's younger residents, but others keep their distance, and there is little to attract the tourist.

The general feeling is that a huge potential has been sacrificed on the altar of the financial services sector, and that what could have been an attractive waterside, on the lines of other successful city waterfronts in Europe,

to indicate when the plane carrying national newspapers had left London and arrived in Jersey.

The signal station closed in 2005 through lack of funding, but a team from the Maritime Museum boat shop still maintains a signal system for strong gales – or flags to mark Liberation Day or Royal birthdays.

Musical entertainment draws a crowd at the Farm and Craft Market in St Helier.

Plain Sailing from St Helier

Cruising around the Jersey coast, racing a catamaran, spotting dolphins or seals, landing mackerel or sea bass or taking a ferry to France are all among the boating options. For visiting offshore reefs and seeing wildlife from a purpose-built rigid inflatable boat, go to www.jerseyseafaris. com. Standard cruise trips in a catamaran along 15 miles (24km) of the south coast depart daily in season from Albert Quay, St Helier. Visit www.jerseycruises. com or go to the booking kiosk at Albert Quay.

Boats can be hired by the hour, day or week.

is just there to provide housing, offices and parking for financiers.

To see for yourself, head south from the slipway, passing the up-turned-boat shaped La Frégate café and the **Jardins de la Mer**. You'll see the towering Radisson Blu Hotel on the Waterfront to the right, and ahead a multiplex cinema, fitness centre and leisure pool. By the time you get to Albert Harbour you might feel like an evening island cruise to see the rather more lovely cliffs and beaches to the west.

Boats moored at Elizabeth Marina.

Eating Out

Banjo
8 Beresford Street; tel: 01534-850 890; www.banjojersey.com; Mon–Sat lunch and dinner.
Part of the Jersey Pottery emporium, Banjo was converted from a former Victorian gentlemen's club and comprises a stylish brasserie and an all-day bar, along with four chic guest rooms on the second floor. ££–£££

Bohemia
Green Street; tel: 01534-880 588; www.bohemiajersey.com; Mon–Fri lunch and dinner, Sat dinner.
The finest food on the island, served in the stylish surroundings of the Club Hotel and Spa, a favourite with celebrities. The chef is Steve Smith, one of the youngest chefs in the UK to achieve a Michelin Star, at the tender age of 24. He fuses tradition with innovation-producing dishes such as roasted scallops with celeriac truffle, apple, smoked eel and a truffle vinaigrette. £££

CaféJac
Jersey Arts Centre, Phillips Street; tel: 01534-879 482; www.cafejac.co.uk; food served Mon–Fri 7.30am–8pm, Sat 8.30am–2.30 pm.
Busy, friendly café where you can turn up any time of day for light bites or full meals. The fluffy pancakes are legendary, and there's a good choice of vegetarian dishes. Tables outside. £

Cock and Bottle
18 Royal Street; tel: 01534-722 184; www.liberationgroup.com; daily 11am–11pm; food served Mon–Thu noon–9pm, Fri–Sat noon–5pm.
Traditional pub with alfresco dining on the square (heaters and blankets provided); perfect on a sunny day to enjoy classic French dishes alongside pub favourites, with chilled wine or a beer. Inside, original 18th-century features have been retained. ££

The Fresh Fish Company
Victoria Pier; tel: 01534-736 799; www.jersey.com/fresh-fish-company; Tue–Sat 8am–2pm, Sun 8am–1pm.
Savour a crab sandwich or lobster claw with a sea view or select fish from the retail shop to grill on a beach BBQ. The company supplies many hotels and restaurants with local fish. ££

The Green Olive
1 Anley Street; tel: 01534-728 198; www.greenoliverestaurant.co.uk; Tue–Fri lunch and dinner, Sat dinner.
Paul Le Brocq's travels have inspired his creative fusion cuisine. Expect a wide range of vegetarian, chicken and seafood dishes, with Mediterranean and Asian flavours. Excellent choice of New World wines. ££

Samphire
7–11 Don Street; tel: 01534-725 100; www.samphire.je; Mon–Fri 9am–late, Sat 10.30am–late
Previously called Ormer, this is an acclaimed restaurant delivering consistently high quality cuisine in a stylish, sophisticated setting. Think foie gras with blood orange and cashew nuts or cauliflower with Romesco sauce, hazelnuts and salsa verde. £££

Tassili
Grand Jersey Hotel, The Esplanade; tel: 01534-722 301; www.handpickedhotels.co.uk; Tue–Sat dinner.
Hotel restaurant noted for its stylish setting and gourmet British cuisine with a decadent Jersey twist. £££

War Tunnels

The preserved tunnel network brings to life the traumatic story of the five years under the Nazi Occupation

A year after the outbreak of World War II Jersey was advertised in the UK press as "the ideal resort for wartime holidays this summer". The Jersey natives never dreamt that just a few weeks later, on 28 June 1940, Germans would be dropping bombs on their island. Within three days the island surrendered and the gruelling five-year German Occupation began.

The Channel Islands were the only territories belonging to Great Britain that fell into German hands during World War II. After the fall of France in 1940 Churchill had decided the cost of the islands' defence could not be justified and they were therefore left undefended. Hitler saw these little islands as the first step to his intended invasion of the United Kingdom. Orders were given in 1941 for Jersey to become an "impregnable fortress".

HO8

Known as Höhlgangsanlage 8, the **Jersey War Tunnels** (Les Charrières Malorey, St Lawrence; Mar–Oct daily 10am–6pm, last admission 4.30pm, Nov Mon-Sun 10am–2.30pm, last admission 1pm) was a massive network of tunnels and galleries, hewn from solid rock with gunpowder and hand tools. Thousands of forced labourers were

One of the unfinished tunnels.

with operating theatre, recovery room and hospital wards.

THE TUNNELS

Ho8 was never to fulfil its role. The occupying forces surrendered on 9 May 1945 and the expected Allied invasion never came. A year later the tunnels were opened to sightseers. The hospital wards were preserved or reconstructed, and the dark, dripping tunnels maintained in their original, unfinished state. A combination of archive film footage, islanders' reminiscences, photos and poignant correspondence chart life under the Nazis. The exhibits bring home the hardship endured by slave labourers (at least 560 died in the Channel Islands), the deprivation of islanders and the fate of those who were deported to camps in Germany. The site also incorporates the Garden of Reflection, designed for visitors to contemplate the suffering endured during the Occupation and the historic War Trail, covering land once used as an artillery battery, and now being reclaimed by nature.

shipped in – later joined by Russian and Ukrainian prisoners of war – who were poorly fed and brutally treated.

The underground centre was originally designed as a subterranean bomb-proof barracks, to store ammunition, fuel and food, and protect the garrison of around 12,000 men against invasion. But the complex was never completed. In the weeks leading to D-Day, with an Allied invasion looming, orders were given for the site to be turned into an emergency casualty receiving station. Five wards were each designed to cope with 100 casualties. Unfinished tunnels were sealed off and the site was equipped

Visitor Information

Jersey War Tunnels, Les Charrières Malorey, St Lawrence; www.jerseywartunnels.com.
Directions: From St Helier follow signs for A1 and The West, and keep on the A1 by branching right at the end of the Esplanade. At Bel Royal turn right onto the A11 and follow the signs for Jersey War Tunnels. Bus route No. 8 Mon–Sat all year, No. 28 from Apr–Sep. Or the special vintage shuttle bus, with commentary, daily every hour from 10.15am–4.15pm departing from Liberation Square, St Helier.

St Aubin's harbour, nestled at the foot of a green valley.

Tour 2

The Southwest

This half-day driving tour covers 11 miles (18km) from St Aubin's Bay to Beauport, where the coast is fringed by the finest beaches on the island

The route follows the coast west from St Helier, via St Aubin, to the southwestern tip of the island. Cliff strolls afford fabulous views, and the choice of beach breaks ranges from big sandy bays with water sports galore to secluded little beaches sheltering below the cliffs. When it comes to restaurants you are spoilt for choice, from the quayside eateries at St Aubin to the string of cafés and fish restaurants right on St Brelade's Bay.

ST AUBIN'S BAY

Leave St Helier via the Esplanade, following the signs for "The West" and St Aubin, keeping to the coast all the way. The gently curving, south-facing St Aubin's Bay stretches for 3 miles (5km) from Elizabeth Castle (see

Highlights

• Picturesque harbour of St Aubin
• St Brelade's Bay
• St Brelade's Parish Church and Fishermen's Chapel
• Beauport Bay

page 25) to St Aubin. The seafront promenade, formerly the route of the Western Railway Line, stretches the entire length of the bay.

During spring tides, giant waves crash over the wall here and sand bags are piled up to protect the small streets leading up from the coastal road. Normally, though, this is a calm, safe bay whose sands are lapped by the shallowest of waters. Prior to the opening

The unique glass interior designed by René Lalique.

Reflected Glory

Halfway round St Aubin's Bay on the A1, St Matthew's Church at Millbrook is known as the Glass Church (Mon–Fri 9am–5pm and for services on Sun). The austere church walls belie a glowing interior that was decorated in opaque glass by the Art Deco glass designer René Lalique. Florence Boot (Lady Trent), the widow of Jesse Boot, founder of Boots the Chemists, commissioned Lalique to embellish the church, then dedicated it to her late husband.

of Jersey's airport in St Peter in 1937, the sands at the eastern end of St Aubin's Bay were used at low tide for take-off and landing of seaplanes flying between the Channel Islands.

Razor fish

When the tide is very low you can have fun trying to catch razor fish (also known as razor clams) in St Aubin's Bay. Go equipped with a bag of salt,

walk along the shoreline and look for the keyhole-shaped burrows in the sand. Sprinkle about a teaspoonful of salt over the hole and wait for around 30 seconds for the razor fish to pop out of its burrow. Hold the clam firmly for a few seconds while it relaxes, then pull it gently out of the hole. The fish are actually long, thin molluscs with cut-throat, razor-like shells. A slightly chewy type of clam, they are

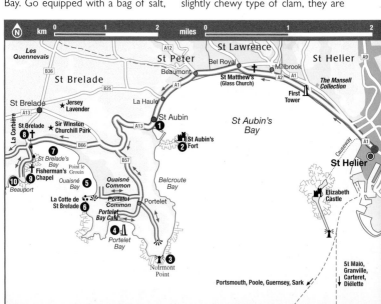

popular in parts of Europe and can be delicious if cooked correctly, ideally steamed with wine, garlic and herbs.

At Bel Royal, where the A1 and A2 converge, keep to the coast road for St Aubin's Harbour. Park just before the harbour, at the main car park on the left hand side of the road.

ST AUBIN

A far smaller, prettier place than St Helier, **St Aubin** ❶ lends itself to quay or seaside strolls and leisurely lunches at inviting alfresco restaurants. The first pier was built in 1675, and a small town subsequently grew up here, with the Bulwarks – the houses beside the harbour – added in 1790. Thanks to its picturesque cottages and its setting at the foot of a green valley, St Aubin was from its earliest days more popular than St Helier.

A haunt of privateers

Named after a 6th-century Breton saint, who was known as a protector against pirates, the town ironically ac-

Picturesque cottages line the harbour at St Aubin.

quired much of its wealth through profiteering (legalised plundering of enemy shipping), and in the 17th and 18th centuries it was the leading port on the island. During the English Civil War many a British vessel was captured and plundered by Sir George Carteret, the Royalist governor of the island. Such were the losses of British ships that Parliamentary forces were sent by Cromwell to put down the Royalist resistance.

Merchants' mansions

Merchants who grew rich on the proceeds of profiteering built themselves fine four-storey houses, often equipped with huge cellars to store the booty. Prior to the construction of the harbour, some of the Bulwarks stood right on the seashore and had spectacular roof outlooks for viewing the return of the fleet. One of the finest still standing is the **Old Court House**, overlooking the harbour, and now a hotel and restaurant. The loot was stored in the cellars and then divided in what was then the Court Room, presided over by the judges.

Fish and ships

Apart from privateering, fortunes were also made by the more honoura-

Originally a wealthy merchant's house, parts of the Old Court House Inn date back to 1450.

ble trades of shipbuilding and cod fishing in Newfoundland. The fishing fleet used to set off across the Atlantic in springtime, returning for the harvest in autumn. The cod were dried, salted and exported, and fishing was the island's most lucrative industry until the late 19th century. Shipowning had also expanded rapidly, and in 1865 Jersey and Guernsey were ranked 10th in British ports. However, the islands were to suffer with the advent of iron steamships in the 1870s. These were too expensive to buy – or build – spelling the end of the great seafaring era.

Today the St Aubin vessels are either jet skis that roar around the bay, motorboats or yachts. The port is home to the **Royal Channel Islands Yacht Club** (you can see it at the end of the quayside), whose first female member was Lillie Lang-

Arts and Crafts

Just across the road from St Aubin's port, the Harbour Gallery (Le Boulevard; daily 10am–5.30pm) is the largest exhibiting and selling gallery in the Channel Islands. Comprising three galleries and a textile centre, it exhibits work from over 80 local artists and craft workers, showcases a minimum of nine exhibitions a year and hosts workshops, classes and events for all ages. Wander at leisure through the galleries and choose from paintings, prints, ceramics, jewellery, woodwork and textiles. It also has an excellent little café.

Original local "works of art" for sale at the Harbour Gallery.

try, one of the most famous figures in Victorian society (see page 82). She was elected a member of the club in 1892.

The Western Railway

Overlooking St Aubin's harbour on the east side is **St Brelade's Parish Hall**, formerly the Terminus Hotel and railway station. The now defunct Western Railway, which linked St Helier to St Aubin, was extended to Corbière in 1884. Trains ran on a single line of standard-gauge track and, apart from delays caused by waves crashing over the sea wall along St Aubin's Bay, the service ran with remarkable efficiency. However, competition from buses and a fire at St Aubin's station, destroying the rolling stock, led to the demise of the service in 1936. The track was turned into a footpath and today makes a delightful 4-mile (6km) walk across the western corner of the island.

Offshore, **St Aubin's Fort ❷** was built to command the western end of the bay in the mid-16th century, predating Elizabeth Castle

(see page 82)

> ### Jersey Birds
>
> Noirmont Point is a critical area for migrant birds; as the most southerly headland in Jersey and the last chance for birds to find food before crossing the open sea to France, it attracts large numbers. Among the less common are honey buzzard, osprey, wryneck, golden oriole, ring ouzel, shorelark, tawny pipit, ortolan and lapland bunting, barred warbler, and melodious warbler. The area was designated an ecological Site of Special Interest in 2007.

at St Helier. Persistent threats of invasion led to additional fortifications over the centuries, the most recent of which were built by the Germans during the Occupation in World War II. You can walk to the fort over the wet sands at low tide, but there is no access to the public as it is now used as a residential sports facility for schools and youth groups; it is only really worth visiting for the views across to St Aubin.

The underground Command Bunker gives a unique insight into German military engineering.

St Aubin's Fort was built in the 1540s to protect shipping in the bay.

Parallel to the coast road, the High Street, known also as **Rue du Crocquet**, used to be the main thoroughfare for horses and carts linking St Aubin with St Helier. Many of the houses were built by wealthy merchants at the end of the 17th century. Those on your right would have backed directly on to the sea, enabling vessels to load and unload. Keep going to the top of the road for fine views across the bay.

St Brelade's Parish Hall is housed in the former railway station.

NOIRMONT POINT

Turn inland from St Aubin along the A13, which climbs up the wooded valley towards St Brelade's Bay. After about a mile (1.6km), turn left on to the B57, the Route de Noirmont, and at the small crossroads, take the left turn just beyond it for **Noirmont Point ❸**. This headland was called "Black Mount" after the clouds that gather over it – said to herald rain. A prominent relic of the Occupation is the huge underground Command Bunker of the former German coast artillery battery, complete with a large observation tower brooding on the clifftop. The bunker has been carefully restored by the Channel Islands German Occupation Society and is open to the public from April to October, most Sundays 11am–4.30pm.

The Coastal Artillery gun to the left of it originally stood at La Coupe, on the northeast coast, but after the war it was thrown over the cliffs by the British, then recovered in 1979.

PORTELET BAY

Return to the junction and turn left for **Portelet Bay ❹**. Park the car at the top of the cliff, by the Old Portelet Inn and admire the views

The sand at Ouaisné Bay is perfect for making sandcastles.

from the top of the cliff. The pretty bay of Portelet below, with its soft, sheltered sands, can be reached by

Portelet Bay is one of the island's most photogenic beaches.

a long flight of steps. The beach is rarely crowded and now has the bonus of a delightful café (see page 45). The little island, accessible at low tide, is properly called the **Île au Guerdain** but more popularly known as Janvrin's Tomb, after the sea captain who was buried here.

When Janvrin was returning with his ship from plague-infested Nantes in France in 1721, he was refused entry to St Aubin's harbour for fear of contamination. Janvrin fell victim himself and, since his body was not allowed ashore, he was given a burial on the island. The body was later transferred to St Brelade's cemetery. The tower on the islet was built over the grave in 1808 as one of the many fortifications against possible invasion during the Napoleonic Wars.

OUAISNÉ BAY

From the Old Portelet Inn, return to the small crossroads, turn left and then take the right fork down to **Ouaisné Bay ❺** (pronounced *Waynay*). The Old Smugglers' Inn, on the left as you go down, is evidence of former activities in this corner of the island.

Île au Guerdain, home to Janvrin's Tomb.

The magnificent sweep of sandy beach, sheltered between headlands, stretches for over a mile, Ouaisné Bay being divided from St Brelade's by a rocky promontory called the Point le Grouin. Even on hot days in high season, Ouaisné's fine sandy beach has plenty of space.

The cliffs south of the bay shelter **La Cotte de St Brelade ⑥** (closed to the public), a major archaeological site excavated on and off for 100 years from 1881. Thirteen teeth of Neanderthal man were discovered here, along with the much older bones of prehistoric woolly mammoth and rhino. These piles of bones, discovered in the 1960s and '70s, suggested that the cave-dwellers stampeded the animals off the cliffs to their deaths.

Behind Ouaisné beach, the gorse-covered common is home to some rare species of fauna. This is the last stronghold of the agile frog, and is also a habitat of the Dartford warbler and the Jersey green lizard. Sightings, however, are rare, and visitors are advised to keep to the pathways and not to disturb the habitat. Protecting Ouaisné Common from the sea and stretching the length of the beach is the German anti-tank wall, built by prisoners during the German Occupation. **Portelet Common**, an expanse of heathland above the beach commanding splendid coastal views, can be reached by the cliff path (see box).

ST BRELADE'S BAY

St Brelade's Bay ⑦ is accessible by foot either across the sands or over

Portelet Common

For dramatic sea views head for the northern edge of Portelet Common, a 77-acre (31-hectare) nature reserve rising 200ft (61 metres) above sea level. From this elevated plateau the view takes in a huge sweep of bay, from Ouaisné below to the far end of St Brelade's Bay. The habitat of gorse, dwarf shrub heathland and lichen grassland supports over 100 plant species, while the crevices of the cliffs provide nesting and roosting sites for shags, oystercatchers and rock pipits.

Sweeping views of St Brelade's Bay from Portelet Common.

The soft sand and safe bathing make sheltered, south-facing St Brelade's one of Jersey's most popular beaches.

the rocky promontory, depending on the tides. To reach the beach by car, return to the junction, joining the A13, then fork left on to the B66 and descend to the bay. With its gently sloping, golden sands, sheltered setting and clear, blue waters St Brelade's is justifiably the most popular beach on the island.

Above the sands, the seafront promenade is bordered by palm-fringed gardens, seafood cafés, souvenir and gift shops. The Sir Winston Churchill Park has immaculate lawns and brightly coloured flowerbeds, while on the slopes above the bay lie some highly desirable tax-exile residences, set in lush south-facing gardens.

The beach is the best equipped on the island, with sun loungers, windbreaks and a whole host of water sports: stand-up paddle boarding, kayaking, coasteering, sailing, water skiing, windsurfing and – when there are waves – surfing and bodyboarding. If you don't fancy getting wet there are plenty of beach activities including beach volleyball and beach football.

When it's time for lunch there is ample choice. You can just step

Seaside Treasure Trove

Design your own glass bead jewellery at Fish 'n' Beads, a quirky little beach shack on the promenade at St Brelade's Bay. There are also funky and original gifts for sale, many of them made from recycled driftwood or other finds washed up on the beach. The hut is open 10am–5pm in summer, check for times rest of year; tel: 01534-742 348.

Creative gifts from recycled driftwood.

straight from the sands to seafood eateries for Jersey oysters and crabs, or a laid-back café for burgers, grills or home-made cakes. The string of cafés and restaurants along the boardwalk all have tables alfresco where you can soak up the stunning sea views.

St Brelade's Church and Fisherman's Chapel

Overlooking the little port at the far end of the bay, the picturesque parish **Church of St Brelade** ❽ dates back to the 12th century and still retains its Norman chancel.

This church was built in pink Jersey granite, and inside you can see pebbles and limpets from the beach embedded in the un-rendered walls.

Nearby, the lovely little **Fisherman's Chapel** ❾ is the oldest place of worship on the island, built in the 11th century on the foundations of an ancient monastic church. The chapel acquired its present name in late medieval times when it was used by the fishing guilds. Having escaped destruction during the Reformation, it was variously used as an armoury, store room and carpenter's shop. In

1880 permission was finally given for the building to revert to a church. Restoration early in the 20th century brought to light the fragments of a series of beautiful medieval frescoes (1375–1425), decorating all four walls. These were restored in 1980, and today the scenes from the Old and New Testaments can be made out with the help of drawings on

Stroll along the Esplanade and gardens at St Brelade's.

The early-Norman Fisherman's Chapel is located beside St Brelade's Church at the western end of the bay.

helpful information boards that reconstruct the missing outlines.

Clearest of all is the scene depicting the *Annunciation* along the east wall. The small kneeling figures either side of the Virgin and Archangel – seven males to the left and seven females to the right – are members of the donor's family.

Fragments of beautiful medieval frescoes decorate the interior of the Fisherman's Chapel.

The flight of granite steps linking the churchyard with the small harbour is the shortest **Perquage** (sanctuary path) on the island. Before the Reformation, criminals who sought refuge in any of the 12 parish churches were allowed to escape via such paths to the safety of a boat and sanctuary in France. Hence each of the parishes has at least a short section of coastline.

Beauport Bay

Take the steep road opposite the main entrance of the churchyard, and turn left for **Beauport** ⑩. Reaching this unspoilt bay entails a longish trek down a bracken-clad cliff – which deters most tourists. Islanders come here, especially at weekends, when sleek yachts are often moored in the bay. There are no facilities on the beach, so take a picnic, and a sunshade or hat.

The clear, still waters are excellent for snorkelling, and children can enjoy fishing in the rock pools.

End the day at **La Corbière** (see page 46), a short drive to the west. This is a dramatic and photogenic spot to watch the sun sink into the Atlantic.

Eating Out

Ouaisné Bay

Kismet Cabana

Ouaisné Car Park, La Rue du Ouaisné, tel: 07700 809 863; www.kismetcabana.com; Sun–Thu 9am–5pm, Fri & Sat 9am–8pm.

Street food inspired by global flavours. This laid-back shack is in Ouaisné Bay's car park but you can take away food to the beach. £

St Aubin's harbour

Lazin Lizard

Mont Les Vaux; tel: 01534-747 740; www.lazinlizard.com; daily 6pm–9.30pm, Sat–Sun also noon–2.30pm.

Buzzy little restaurant catering for all tastes with tasty dishes like crispy squid, Jamaican Jerk chicken, sticky ribs and steak with teriyaki prawns. ££

Salty Dog Bar and Bistro

Le Boulevard; tel: 01534-742 760; www.saltydogbistro.com; dinner daily, lunch Tue–Sun (Fri–Sun off-season).

Relaxed alfresco dining and food that is big on flavour, freshness and spice. Cocktails and contemporary music are part of the scene. £££

St Peter

Mark Jordan at the Beach

La Plage, La Route de la Haule; tel: 01534-780 180; www.markjordanatthebeach.com; lunch and dinner daily.

Run by the same chef as the Ocean Restaurant in the Atlantic Hotel (see page 124) this casual bistro on the beachside promenade offers high quality, simple cuisine with the emphasis on fish. ££–£££

Portelet Bay

Portelet Bay Café

Portelet Bay; tel: 01534-728 550; www.porteletbaycafe.com; daily from 10am, lunch and dinner.

Family-run café right on the beach with quirky upcycled decor. Delicious wood-fired pizzas and the catch of the day is brought in by boat. A lovely scenic spot, worth the trek down from the Portelet Headland (no car access). Booking essential in summer. ££

The Old Smugglers' Inn

Le Mont de Ouaisné; tel: 01534-741 510; www.oldsmugglersinn.com; daily 11am–11pm, food served noon–2pm and 6–9pm.

Popular pub, close to the beach, converted from 17th-century cottages. Traditional pub food. £

St Brelade's Bay

Crab Shack

Tel: 01534-850 855; www.jerseycrabshack.com; Apr–Sep Mon lunch, Tue–Sun lunch and dinner; Oct–Mar closed all day Mon and dinner on Sun.

Rustic beachfront eatery that's all about the seafood; from home-made mackerel pâté and local crab bisque to Jersey oysters and freshly picked spider crab, all beautifully presented. £–££

Oyster Box

La Route de la Baie; tel: 01534-850 888; www.oysterbox.co.uk; Tue–Sun lunch and dinner.

Mainly seafood restaurant with a great location on the bay. The menu stretches across the culinary spectrum from gourmet burgers to Jersey oysters, crab and lobster. Seaside terrace. ££–£££

Wayside Café

Le Mont Sohier; tel: 01534-743 915; daily 9am–9pm.

The locals' favourite seaside café, with a large terrace overlooking the beach and a menu to suit all tastes. Hearty breakfasts, home-made puddings, sizzling grills, salads, seafood and daily specials. £–££

The dramatic rocky headland and La Corbière lighthouse.

Tour 3

The West Coast

This half-day driving tour of 14 miles (22km) takes in Jersey's most dramatic coast, where surfers ride the big Atlantic swell on a spectacular 4-mile (6km) beach

The wild and windswept bay of St Ouen's dominates the entire coast. This is a surfers' paradise, with championship-size waves and Bondi Beach-style lifeguards on patrol. On the landward side, Les Mielles is the largest remaining area of unspoilt countryside on the island, its sanddune system rich in flora and fauna.

Highlights

- La Corbière lighthouse
- St Ouen's Bay
- La Rocco
- Channel Islands Military Museum

LA CORBIÈRE

Marking the southwestern tip of the island is **La Corbière ❶**, or haunt of the crow, once considered a bird of ill omen. This is a wild and desolate corner, abounding in tales of ships that have foundered on the treacherous rocks and sailors who have drowned. The first recorded disaster on the rocks here was a Spanish vessel car-

rying a cargo of wine in 1495. Among the many other shipwrecks was the Royal Mail Steam Packet in 1859.

However, it was not until 1874 that a lighthouse, the first in the British Isles to be made of concrete, was built here. Perched on jagged rocks and often lashed by waves, this makes a dramatic scene at any time of day. There are still occasional accidents here, the most recent involving a French catamaran, en route from Jer-

Anti-Tank Walls

The 6ft (2-metre) -thick concrete wall along the entire bay of St Ouen's was one of many anti-tank walls which were built by the Germans on the Channel Islands. Orders had been given to transform the island into 'an impregnable fortress', and thousands of foreign forced labourers and Russian prisoners-of-war were imported to construct the walls, gun emplacements, artillery batteries and bunkers. Over half a million tons of concrete were used around the coasts, with narrow-gauge railways built specifically for its transport.

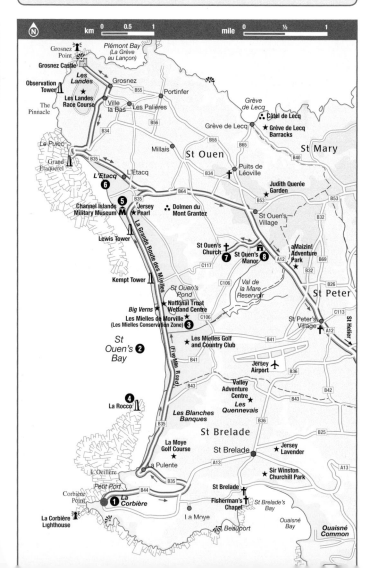

A World War II coastal defence gun at La Corbière.

sey to Sark, which struck a rock north of the lighthouse in 1995. The sculpted pair of clasped hands on the headland commemorates the rescue of all 307 passengers and crew.

If the tide is right, you can walk across the causeway to the lighthouse, but the incoming sea is treacherous, and you should check the tides before setting out. A

The granite memorial at La Corbière pays tribute to a successful sea rescue.

carved stone on the causeway recalls the fate of an assistant lighthouse keeper who drowned while trying to save a visitor stranded by the incoming tide. Nowadays a siren warns visitors when the tide approaches the causeway.

Originally manned by four keepers, the lighthouse today is remotely operated, and there is no access inside for visitors. During World War II the Germans built bunkers at La Corbière and a great grey observation tower on the clifftop overlooking the lighthouse. This was used as a radio tower and, more recently, converted by Jersey Heritage into self-catering accommodation, in German modernist Bauhaus style. The tower is over six floors and commands a wonderful 360-degree panorama of the island from the top.

ST OUEN'S BAY

For **St Ouen's Bay** ❷ to the north, continue around the headland, passing above the rocky Petit Port Bay, and in about a mile (1.6km) turn left on to the B35. The longest bay in the Channel Islands, the swathe of sands stretches in a great 4-mile

Concrete observation tower at La Corbière.

(6km) arc, all the way from La Pulente in the south to L'Etacq in the north. This is a beach which is never crowded.

Surfers' paradise
Throughout the year surfers make the most of the rollers on the incoming tides. Bodyboarding is hugely popular too. Surfboards, body boards, skim boards and wetsuits can be all hired at various points along the beach or, for those who prefer just to sit and watch the action, the sea wall affords shelter, and there are occasional cafés above the beach with sea-view terraces. Elsewhere the beach is very exposed and not ideal for sunbathing; and when the weather is inclement, the bay is far from welcoming. All but experienced surfers should heed the danger warnings and keep to the areas between the flags where lifeguards are on duty during summer. The bay is notorious for rip tides and strong currents.

The most sheltered section is **La Pulente** in the south, where, at the right tide, children can enjoy sandy pools in the rocky outcrops.

Les Mielles
The main road skirting the bay, La Grande Route des Mielles, is also known as Five Mile Road. On foot it may feel like at least 5 miles (8km), but it is in fact less than 4 miles (6km). On the landward side, the sand dunes of **Les Mielles Conservation Zone ❸** are the habitat of a wide range of birds and plants, including several endangered species. **La Mare au Seigneur**, colloquially known as St Ouen's Pond, was, until World War II, used to stock fish for the Seigneur of St Ouen, and the reeds used for thatching and bed-

On the Crest of the Waves
The first stand-up surfers in Jersey were a group of South Africans who, in the 1950s, saw film footage of St Ouen's in an advertisement for the island in a UK cinema. Inspired by the bay they moved to Jersey, set up as lifeguards here and taught the islanders the art of stand-up surfing. The sport quickly caught on and the Jersey Surfboard Club – one of the oldest in Europe – was founded in 1959.

Head down to St Ouen's for guaranteed high rollers.

ding. The land was purchased by the National Trust for Jersey in 1972 and is now a nature reserve. A rich diversity of flora surrounds the pond, and the nearby field called **Le Noir Pré** or 'The Orchid Field' is one of the last strongholds of the Jersey or loose-flowered orchid *(Orchis laxiflora)*, providing a blaze of colour in May and June.

The reed beds and marshy surrounds of the pond attract a large variety of birds. Since 1992, 188 species have been recorded at the site and, with changes in climate, an increasing number are arriving each year. Among the breeding birds are Cetti's warbler, reed and sedge warblers, bearded tit and reed bunting. A pair of marsh harriers bred here for the first time in 2002, and the species can often be spotted soaring overhead. The National Trust's Jersey Wetland Centre (May–Sept daily 7am–7pm) has panoramic views of the reed bed and pond, and is equipped with binoculars and a live-feed reed bed cam. Access is via a tunnel, entered on La Grande Route des Mielles (park at the Watersplash, cross the road, and it's just to the north).

Lewis Tower, built in 1835 to defend Jersey's coast.

A large part of the land running alongside Five Mile Road is given over to golf courses, including Les Mielles Golf and Country Club, which also has an activity centre with lots of things to entertain children, including minigolf and a fun zone.

Coastal towers

At the southern end of the bay, out to sea, **La Rocco ❹** tower is the oldest of nine towers which were built to

La Rocco tower was badly damaged during the Occupation.

Sea-holly can be found in the sand dunes near St Ouen's Bay.

defend the bay during the Napoleonic Wars. Damaged by German target shooting during the Occupation, the tower underwent renovation in 1969. Only three of the other towers survive, including **Kempt Tower** (1834) on the seafront further north. This is one of the few surviving examples of a Martello tower. The ground floor was used to store weapons and armour; the upper floor housed the troops. Today the tower provides self-catering accommodation for up to 12 people.

At the north end of the bay, **Lewis Tower** stands on the site where the local rector set up a cannon in 1779, in anticipation of the capture of the island by the adventurer, the Prince of Nassau, with a French force of 6,000. The invasion was repulsed by the Jersey Militia and the French warships were forced to return to St Malo, where five of the boats were destroyed by the British. The structure you see today is a Martello tower of 1835. This was used by the Germans in World War II, who constructed an extension at the base to house a searchlight.

For centuries *vraic* (pronounced 'rack') or seaweed from the beach has been collected for use as a fertiliser on the farmland bordering the coast.

Horses and carts were once used for the job, gaining access to the beaches via slipways which you can see all the way around the Jersey coastline. In 1600 laws were passed to guarantee farmers equal rights to the free fertiliser. Today it is a free-for-all but nowadays you rarely see tractors going down to collect the vraic.

Knitting traditions

Follow La Grande Route des Mielles to the end of the main beach for the Château complex and the former **Jersey Woollen Mills**.

Seaweed is harvested in St Ouen's Bay and used as a fertiliser.

Knitting is one of the islands' oldest traditions, and records date back to the 16th century when women would knit sweaters to keep their menfolk warm on their long journeys to the cod banks in Newfoundland.

Jersey became famous for the trade, and knitted goods, especially stockings and waistcoats, were exported to England and France. According to the records of an early 17th-century Lieutenant Bailiff of Jersey, the majority of the islanders (children included) were knitters, and over 10,000 pairs of stockings were produced weekly. The noise of knitting needles during sermons became so prominent that vicars put a stop to knitting inside the church.

The harvest and *vraicing* (seaweed collection) began to suffer and in 1608, in order to encourage more workers onto the land, an act was passed prohibiting those over the age of 15 from knitting during the harvest. The penalty was imprisonment.

Each jersey made on the Channel Islands had its own distinctive style. Legend has it that if a sailor was lost at sea and his body washed ashore, he would be identified by his sweater and returned to his native parish.

L'Etacq is a small community just a few hundred metres inland.

An elegant freshwater pearl necklace on display at Jersey Pearl.

Sadly, these days, jerseys are no longer made on the island.

Channel Islands Military Museum

A restored German bunker, sitting on the seafront next to Lewis Tower, is home to the **Channel Islands Military Museum** ❺ (mid-Apr–Oct daily 10am–5pm). The bunker is limited in space but is packed with fascinating military and civilian memorabilia from the German Occupation.

Apart from anti-aircraft guns, soldiers in uniform and military motorcycles, there is a rare Enigma decoding machine, a series of Red Cross letters to relations and friends in England and Christmas and birthday cards made by Jersey internees at the Worzach and Bieberach camps in southern Germany. Orders of the Commandant include a notice of a Jersey resident, Louis Berrier, being charged with espionage for releasing a pigeon messenger for England. He was court-martialled and executed.

Relics of Red Cross food parcels that arrived by ship towards the end of the German Occupation include tins of dried egg. Food was severely rationed during the Occupation, but the islanders

The Channel Islands Military Museum is housed in a coastal defence bunker which formed part of Hitler's Atlantic war defences.

were resourceful, creating coffee from parsnips, tea from peapods and tooth-paste from crushed cuttlefish and ivy.

Another tourist attraction of a different nature is **Jersey Pearl** (daily 9am–5pm), just across the main road.. In this spacious, plush showroom you can watch pearl-threading, have your own necklace made or choose from a wide range of cultured, freshwater or simulated pearls.

The main road heads inland after Jersey Pearl. The B35 takes you to

L'Etacq ❻, a vast expanse of reefs better suited to rock pool exploring than swimming. A forest close to L'Etacq was submerged when the sea level rose after the Ice Age, and on rare occasions when the sands have been washed away by storms you can see the remains of ancient tree stumps. At the far end of the bay, and accessible by road, an old German bunker sells lobster, crabs, prawns and fresh fish. For a gourmet picnic, order ready-cooked lobster (Faulkner Fisheries; tel:

German Relics

Instead of destroying the conspicuous evidence of an unhappy episode in its history, Jersey retained its German relics after World War II. Apart from becoming tourist attractions, they have been put to good use. The sea wall along St Ouen acts as a barrier against the Atlantic, one of the bunkers is home to the Channel Islands Military Museum, another a retail outlet for freshly caught lobsters, while the six-storey, sea-view observation tower at Corbière has been converted for holiday lets.

A World War II German pistol displayed in the Channel Islands Military Museum.

Faulkner Fisheries in L'Etacq, at the northern end of St Ouen's Bay, supply many major Jersey restaurants with fresh seafood.

01534-483 500; Mon 8am–2pm (but BBQ closed), Tues-Sat 8am-5pm, BBQ noon–3pm) or enjoy delicious and affordable barbecued seafood at wooden benches overlooking the coast Don't be put off by the occasional bad odour on the coast here – it's only accumulated weed from Le Pulec to the north – familiarly known as Stinky Beach.

To enjoy some spectacular views from castle ruins you could head

aMaizin!

At La Houge Farm, St Peter, Jersey's aMaizin! Adventure Park (tel: 01534-482 116; www.jerseyleisure.com) has ample to entertain the kids: a toboggan run, pedal-karts, tractor rides, hands-on craft activities, a new indoor fun zone, animals and, from July to mid-September, a maze constructed entirely of the cereal crop. The maze is planted in April, plotted by GPS in May, plucked in June and opened in July. Finally in September, it is cut down and passed to a local farmer for feed. Puzzles and clues in the labyrinth provide fun for all the family – and there is also a mini-maze for little ones with only five clues that is accessible to buggies.

on north up to **Grosnez** (see page 78) on the north coast – a diversion of approximately 3 miles (5km). Otherwise retrace your steps along the B35 and join the B64 to reach the village of **St Ouen**.

The **parish church of St Ouen ❼** is one of the finest on the island, and lies southwest of the actual village, on the crest of a hill overlooking the sea. To get there take the A12, then the C117 marked to the right. Notably, the church was mentioned in a charter signed by William the Conqueror prior to his conquest of England. Major alterations and extensions took place between the 12th and 19th centuries. The original building, possibly a chantry chapel erected by a group of monks from Normandy in the 7th century, is thought to have been rebuilt or enlarged by a member of the historic de Carteret family, Seigneurs of St Ouen, whose nearby ancient seat can be seen from the main A12.

The magnificent **Manor of St Ouen ❽** (closed to the public), owned by the family for more than 800 years, was used by the German army during the Occupation. Inside the grounds, the Chapel of St Anne, built at the same time as the manor, was turned into a storeroom and

butcher's shop. The manor is now a
popular wedding venue.

The next village along the A12 is **St
Peter's**, whose parish church has the
tallest spire on the island and so flash-
es a warning red light for planes landing and taking off from the nearby airport. A church has stood on this site
for over 1,000 years, like St Ouen's,
pre-dating the Conquest. It has some
unusual stained glass windows, including one about the airport.

Return to St Helier by continuing
south along the A12 and turning left
on to the A1 when you come to the
main junction.

Parts of St Ouen's parish church may
predate 1066.

Eating Out

St Ouen's Bay
Big Vern's
La Grande Route des Mielles; tel:
01534-481 705; daily breakfast, lunch
and dinner until 9pm or 6pm off
season.
Overlooking the rollers of St Ouen's
Bay, this is the favourite restaurant
of local surfers. Choose from lobster
or sea bass, home-baked ham, free-
range chicken, veggie burgers, steak
or salads. Light and airy with plenty of
outdoor seating but be prepared to
queue. ££
El Tico Beach Cantina
La Grande Route des Mielles; tel:
01534-482 009; www.elticojersey.
com; breakfast, lunch and dinner daily
until 8.30pm.
A familiar landmark of St Ouen's Bay,
and a favourite surfers' haunt. The
original café here dated back to 1948
but was rebuilt a few years ago in
swish Art Deco style. It caters for all
tastes and is a great spot to watch the
waves roll in. ££
The Koru Arms at La Pulente
La Route de la Pulente; tel: 01534-
744 487; daily 11am–11pm, food

served daily noon–2.30pm and
6–8/9pm.
At the southern end of St Ouen's,
this is a friendly pub offering steaks,
burgers and seafood as well as pre-
surf breakfasts. It's also a great spot
to watch the sunset over the Five
Mile beach. £
Le Braye
La Grande Route des Mielles; tel:
01534-481 395; www.lebraye.com;
summer Mon–Sat 9am–9pm, Sun
9am–8pm; shorter hours off-season.
Gaze across the huge bay of
St Ouen's and stoke up on big
breakfasts before hitting the waves.
Or come for crustaceans, Jersey beef
or veggie burgers or Jersey cream
teas. This is one of the safer areas
for swimming at St Ouen's so it's very
popular with families. £
Ocean Restaurant
Atlantic Hotel, La Mont de la
Pulente; tel: 01534-744 101; www.
theatlantichotel.com; breakfast, lunch
and dinner daily.
Enjoy sublime views of St Ouen's Bay
and award-winning cuisine based on
the finest Jersey produce. £££

Fables and Festivals

Jersey abounds with myth, superstition and strange customs. Prehistoric menhirs and dolmens gave rise to devil worship and witchcraft, and stormy seas sowed the seeds of legend

Many are the tales of wreckers who lured ships onto the treacherous reef of La Corbière by burning fires near the rocks, indicating a safe haven from the stormy waters. The invariable shipwreck would bring death to the crew and precious cargo to the fishermen.

Medieval legend tells the story of the dragon of St Lawrence, who terrorised the islanders and who was slain by Lord of Hambye from Normandy.

On the north coast tales were told of the *Black Dog of Bouley Bay*, a terrifying creature with huge saucer eyes that roamed the coastline of the bay.

Some islanders are still superstitious. Legend has it that anyone who witnesses cattle on bended knees on Christmas Eve (in other words, worshipping) will die before the year is out. Several of the old farmers still make sure their cattle are bedded well before the midnight hour.

Among Jersey's ancient customs is *les visites du branchage*, the twice-yearly inspections by parish officials to check that no boughs or bushes encroach on roads and footpaths. Fines can be levied on landowners who fail to keep their hedges in trim.

Jersey International Air Display.

parade of spectacular floral floats. Competition between the parishes is fierce.

Festivals and Events

For full listings go to www.jersey. com or tel: 01534-859 000.

Liberation Day: 9 May. Islanders celebrate the liberation from the German forces on 9 May 1945. Heritage Festival: March-May. Events, re-enactments, special openings and activities with historical themes take place around all the Channel Islands and are timed to coincide with Liberation Day (see above), but are spread over several weeks.

Jersey Food Festival: late May. A five-day celebration of Jersey's food, providing a showcase for local producers, chefs and restaurateurs. Masterclasses plus farm and dairy tours.

June in Bloom: end June. Four-day floral festival with tours, talks and workshops.

Battle of Flowers: second Thursday in August followed on the Friday by the Illuminated Moonlight Parade with selected floats and bands.

Jersey Film Festival: second week of August. Free nightly films in Howard Davis Park

Gorey Fête: third week in August. Beach events, fairground rides.

International Air Display: second week of September.

Tennerfest: six weeks from October to mid-November. Dining from £10 at over 100 restaurants.

La Fête de Noué: December. Christmas festival. Street entertainment, parades and markets in St Helier.

BATTLE OF FLOWERS

Of all Jersey's festivals, the biggest crowd-puller is the **Battle of Flowers**. The first "Battle" took place in 1902 on Victoria Avenue, St Helier, to celebrate the Coronation of King Edward VII. With the exception of World War I and the German Occupation, the event has been held here every year since. Formerly the flowers were ripped out of the floats and a real battle of flowers ensued. Nowadays the entertainment is provided by marching bands, dancers, beauty queens headed by Miss Jersey and a celebrity Mr Battle – all accompanying the

Spectacular swathes of lavender at Jersey Lavender Farm.

Tour 4

Flowers and Farming

Full of botanical and rural delights, this whole-day driving tour of 14 miles (22km) takes you to a heritage museum, vineyards, watermills and a fragrant lavender farm

A way from the coast you'll find a surprisingly unspoilt landscape of valleys, woods, country lanes and farming land. Agriculture is no longer a main source of income for Jersey, but farming is still a way of life for at least some of the islanders. Half of the land is agricultural, and the sunny south-facing slopes yield Jersey Royal potatoes and tomatoes, while the famous Jersey cow provides islanders with milk, cream and butter.

The temperate climate, long hours of sunshine and rich soil make Jersey a gardener's paradise. Each year the island puts on a programme of open gardens, demonstrations, flower shows and environmental walks. Flowers are grown both for export and for the decoration of floats at Jersey's cel-

Highlights

- Waterworks Valley
- Hamptonne Country Life Museum
- Tour and tastings at La Mare Wine Estate
- Jersey Lavender

ebrated Battle of Flowers. The island is also famous for its orchids, both wild and cultivated, as well as other species of rare wild flowers. During the August summer flower show the **Royal Jersey Horticultural Society** (www.royaljersey.co.uk) arranges four shows a year with some spectacular floral and vegetable displays.

Owners of private gardens occasionally open their gates to the public

Hedge Veg

When you're driving along the lanes inland you may come across fresh produce (especially Jersey Royals) sold at roadside stalls outside farms and private houses. You choose what you want and leave the correct change in an honesty box. You used to see them everywhere but now many have been replaced by the growing number of farm shops.

Cash and carry along the country lanes.

on Sundays at other times of year. For information visit www.jersey.com.

BATTLE OF FLOWERS

From St Helier, follow the signs for 'The West' and the A1, taking you along the Esplanade. This becomes Victoria Avenue, venue of the annual Battle of Flowers which takes place every August and features bands, celebrities and a long parade of spectacular floats made of flowers. Tickets can be purchased online at www.battleofflowers.com.

Apart from breaks during World War I and the German Occupation in World War II, the event has taken place every year since 1902, when the first 'Battle' celebrated the Coronation of King Edward VII. It is one of the largest floral carnivals in Europe.

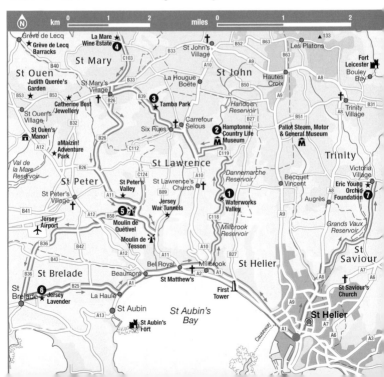

The cluster of faithfully restored buildings at Hamptonne Country Life Museum capture the spirit of rural Jersey.

A day or two before the event volunteers can be seen busily cutting blooms and gluing them to the floats, though these days many are made of paper. If you happen to miss the Battle of Flowers, some of these amazing creations can be seen displayed around the parishes for a few days following the event.

Before the 1960s it really *was* a battle, with floats being stripped and both participants and onlookers pelting each other with flowers. Nowadays the floats remain intact, and

A *goodwyf* gives you the latest 17th-century farming gossip.

it's more about marching bands and beauty queens. The event takes place on the second Thursday in August, with an illuminated Moonlight Parade the evening after.

WATERWORKS VALLEY

When the road divides, follow signs for the A1 which take you along the inner coastal road. Keep to this road until you see a turning to the right with a small sign for **Waterworks Valley ❶** (C118). The road twists up through the lush green valley. This is one of Jersey's loveliest natural features, with leafy glades and woodland paths. The stream here used to power six watermills — hence the original name of the road, 'Le Chemin des Moulins'. The late 19th century saw the construction of the 3-mile (5km) long Millbrook reservoir, followed later by the Dannemarche and Handois reservoirs to the north, giving the valley its somewhat pedestrian name.

HAMPTONNE COUNTRY LIFE MUSEUM

Beyond the Dannemarche Reservoir, fork left (on the C119) to get

Traditional apple press in the cider barn at Hamptonne.

vated as the homes of farming families of the 17th and 18th centuries.

The newly refurbished Syvret House gives an insight into 1940s rural life including farming traditions, day-to-day family life, language, religion and the German Occupation.

The nearby cider barn *(pressoir)* houses the apple crusher and twin-screw apple press that are still used every autumn to make cider. During La Faîs'sie d'Cidre (Cider Festival) in mid-October you can see the cider being made in the old-fashioned way, with a horse crushing the apples and the juice then extracted on the press.

This is very much a living museum, often with a farmer's wife *(goodwyf* in the Jersey patois) in period costume to tell you tales of the English Civil War or the latest gossip from the 17th-century farming community; or you might find a spinner or lace-maker demonstrating bygone skills. Youngsters can follow a nature trail, meet the Hamptonne piglets and calves or test their knowledge with activity sheets or puzzles in the Children's Room.

to the **Hamptonne Country Life Museum ②** (La Rue de la Patente; www.jerseyheritage.org; late May–mid-Sept daily 10am–5pm), which is tucked away in a lovely rustic setting, surrounded by gardens, meadows and woodland.

The group of farmhouses and outbuildings has been restored to demonstrate 300 years of the island's rural heritage. The interiors of the two oldest houses have been reno-

Pallot Museum

This fascinating collection of steam and farm machinery, motor vehicles, vintage bikes and organs was put together by the late Don Pallot, a talented Jersey engineer. He invented farming implements to facilitate life for Jersey farmers, among them the Pallot Elevator Digger and the Last Furrow Reversible Plough. On Thursdays you can travel in a Victorian steam-drawn coach. (Located east of Hamptonne, off the A9 on Rue du Bechet, Trinity; www.pallotmuseum.co.uk; Apr–Oct Mon–Sat 10am–5pm.

A Jersey builder's truck; a 1931 Chevrolet 30 cwt lorry.

Make sure you stop at the café (see page 67) run by Jersey Kitchen, and serving genuine Jersey food.

TAMBA PARK

Descending the road from the Hamptonne Museum, turn right at the junction, then left and first right down a narrow lane for the A10. Turn right and at the Carrefour Selous junction bear left on to the B39 and follow the road until you come to **Tamba Park** ❸ (indoor area daily 9am–6pm, outdoor area 10am–5pm, off-season 10am-dusk; www.tambaexperience.co.uk). If you have youngsters in tow they will find plenty of entertainment at Jersey's newest attraction, especially the Dino Trail with its life-size animated dinosaurs. Kids can also enjoy the adventure play zone, the fish-feeding area and the micro boats. For garden lovers there are extensive grounds with an ornamental lake and sculpture garden. All profits from Tamba Park go to Ruff's Kitchens, a charity run by the own-ers of the park which sets up kitchens in schools in Zimbabwe to feed malnourished children.

LA MARE WINE ESTATE

Continue along the B39 as far as St Mary's Village and then follow the signs along the C103 towards the Devil's Hole and **La Mare Wine Estate** ❹ (www.lamarewineestate. com; Apr–Nov daily 10am–5pm). From a small vineyard La Mare has grown into one of Jersey's main tourist attractions, as well as a wedding and corporate venue. The 25-acre (10-hectare) wine estate produces red, white and sparkling wines as well as Jersey gin and vodka made from Jersey Royals. Guided tours of the vineyards, winery, distillery and chocolate kitchen include tastings along the way.

The sparkling wines are made according to the *méthode champenoise* – Jersey is on the same degree of latitude as Champagne; they also make a sparkling cider, apple brandy, along with jams, marmalades, jellies and Jer-

Dino Trail at Tamba Park.

Carousel at Tamba Park.

sey black butter (a type of preserve, not a butter).

If you don't make it to La Mare itself you can always purchase their products from the Maison La Mare in King Street, St Helier.

ST PETER'S VALLEY

Return to St Mary's Village and take the B26, signed to **St Peter's Val-**

A sparkling wine selection from La Mare Wine Estate.

ley. This will eventually join the A11, which continues through this lovely green valley – it was here that Queen Victoria was brought when she asked to see the most beautiful spot on the island. The valley was the site of six watermills, used mainly for grinding flour.

Turn right on to the B58, just over a mile along the A11, to see the only surviving fully working mill on the island, the **Moulin de Quétivel ⑤** (Mont Fallu; www.nationaltrust.je; May–mid-Sept Sat 10am–4pm). A mill has operated here intermittently since feudal times, the current one dating from the 18th century. Abandoned in the early 20th century, it was revived by the Germans during the Occupation, only to fall into disrepair again. It was eventually brought back to working order by the National Trust in 1979.

The top floor has an exhibition on the history of milling, while the first and ground floors demonstrate how the mill works. There is a shop selling freshly ground organic flours and a wide range of locally produced gifts and a film showing how cabbage loaves (still sold in some bakeries on the island) are made in gorse ovens.

Daily guided tours with tastings will take you through the vineyards, orchards and distillery of La Mare Wine Estate.

Although the mill is open only on Mon & Tues (May-Sept, 10am-4pm), you can park here at any time and take the footpath from the mill to the

Moulin de Quétivel is the only working mill left in St Peter's Valley, and still grinds its own flour.

mill pond, through red squirrel-inhabited woodland.

Lower down, at the entrance of St Peter's Valley, **Le Moulin de Tesson** (Tesson Mill, same opening times as Moulin de Quétivel), has been restored by the National Trust. There has probably been a mill on the site since the 11th century. To fund the restoration of the water-wheel and steam-engine room the National Trust had to grant a long lease to convert the interior to residential apartments. A short film relates the history of the mill.

JERSEY LAVENDER

Continuing on the B58, go straight over the next crossroads for the A12. Turn left here and right at the roundabout which bypasses the airport and brings you into St Brelade. Just after the Quennevais shopping precinct turn left along the B25, signposted to **Jersey Lavender ⑥** (www.jersey lavender.co.uk; early May–Sept Tue–Sun 10am–5pm). The fields of lavender, covering 9 acres (4 hectares), provide a Provence-like blaze of purple throughout the summer. This is a family-owned and -run business that

For plant-lovers, there are over 60 varieties of lavender on view at Jersey Lavender, and most are for sale.

was set up in the 1980s. The garden contains around 60 different varieties of lavender, plus dozens of culinary, medicinal, aromatic and dyers' herbs. The lavender is cut by hand, distilled on site and the essential oils matured and blended with other ingredients to produce eau de toilette, colognes, soap, lotions and lavender bags. A video presentation shows all the stages of production and during the harvest season (June–mid-August) talks are given on the distillation process at 11.30am and 3pm.

The best time to visit is early June to late July/early August – the *lavandage* or lavender harvest is usually over by mid-August, but visitors can still watch the distilling and bottling processes and purchase products

Jersey National Trust

If you're a member of the National Trust, make sure you take your card when you go to Jersey. The island has its own National Trust (www.nationaltrust.je) dedicated to preserving sites of historic, aesthetic and natural interest. It is the largest private land owner on Jersey, maintaining over 130 sites. Admission to the sites is free for NT members on production of a membership card. The organisation has a year-round programme of free, themed guided walks; collect a leaflet from the National Trust office at The Elms, La Chève Rue, in St Mary for further details.

The Jersey National Trust was founded in 1936.

Judith Querée's Garden

Plant enthusiasts should not miss an opportunity to take a tour of Judith Querée's Garden, set in a peaceful valley in the parish of St Ouen and encircling a 350-year old traditional Jersey granite cottage. It is only just over 0.25 acres (0.1 hectares) in size but it manages to pack in around 2,000 (mainly herbaceous) perennials from all over the world, many of them rare and unusual. Judith gives personal guided tours of her award-winning garden by appointment (May-Sept, 11am or 2pm on Tue, Wed or Thur). The full address is:Creux Baillot Cottage, Le Chemin des Garennes, Leoville; www.judithqueree.com. Telephone in advance for access details: 01534-482 191. Not suitable for young children.

made from the lavender essence. Further attractions are the herb garden, woodland walk and Sprigs Café (see page 67) where lavender finds its way into a number of sweet and savoury dishes.

To return to St Helier take the B25 eastwards and join the main coastal road back to St Helier.

DETOUR TO ERIC YOUNG ORCHID FOUNDATION

Floral enthusiasts should not leave Jersey without a visit to the **Eric Young Orchid Foundation** ❼ (Victoria Village; www.ericyoungorchidfoundation.co.uk; Feb–mid-Dec Wed–Sat 10am–4pm), tucked away in the heart of the countryside in the parish of Trinity. From St Helier take the ring road, following signs to 'The North', then turn off for the A8 to Trinity. After half a mile, turn right, following signposts for Les Grands Vaux and the Orchid Foundation. The road takes you past Les Grands Vaux reservoir, then to Victoria Village, where the Foundation is signposted to the left.

The late Eric Young devoted his life to breeding new hybrids of orchid, and his exhibitions won prestigious awards. He first established a collection in Jersey in 1958, and within a decade it was recognised as one of the leading private collections in Europe and eight times winner of the Chelsea Flower Show Gold Award. Young's ambition to set up an orchid foundation open to the public was achieved, but he died in 1984 at the age of 73, before the project was completed.

The fruits of his lifelong efforts can be seen in the growing houses where exotic orchids of dazzling colours are set against a backdrop of ponds, branches, rocks and raised beds.

There is a dazzling display of orchids on show at the Eric Young Orchid Foundation.

Immerse yourself in exotic orchid blooms at the Eric Young Orchid Foundation.

Eating Out

St Aubin's Bay
The Lookout Beach Café
First Tower, Victoria Avenue; tel: 01534-616 886; Mon–Sat 9am–9pm, Sun 9am–8pm.
Between St Helier and St Aubin, with views across the bay of St Aubin, this café has plenty of family favourites as well as dishes of the day in summer based on available fresh ingredients. Think sea bass with dauphinoise potatoes, hand-dived scallops with pancetta and tempura calamari with fries. £–££

St Mary
Vineyard Café
La Mare Wine Estate; tel: 01534-484 536; www.lamarewineestate.com; Apr–Oct daily 10am–4.30pm.
Look out on to neat rows of vines and enjoy light lunches or Jersey cream teas with home-made jams from the estate. £–££

St Peter's Valley
Victoria in the Valley
La Vallée de St Pierre, near Moulin de Quétival; tel: 01534-485 498; daily 11am–11pm, food served Tue–Sat noon–2pm and 6–8.30pm, Sun 2–4.30pm.
A friendly pub with draught and cask ales, reasonably priced pub grub, alfresco seating with garden views and log fires in winter. £–££

St Brelade
Sprigs Café
Jersey Lavender Farm, Rue du Pont Marquet; tel: 01534-742 933; www.jerseylavender.co.uk; Apr–Sep Tue–Sun 10am–5pm.
Light lunches and a range of home-made cakes and scones. Try the lavender scone with Jersey butter and cream, the honey and lavender ice cream or the delicious honey-roast ham served with lavender jelly. £

The Tree House
La Marquanderie Hill; tel: 01534-741 177; www.theboathousegroup.com; lunch and dinner daily.
Authentic Italian using Jersey's only fully wood-burning oven to produce scrumptious crispy base pizzas in a lovely forest setting. Indoor and outdoor play areas, crazy golf and soft play area for little ones. ££

Boats at Bonne Nuit Bay.

J 258

Tour 5

The North Coast

No visit to Jersey is complete without a tour of the dramatic northern coastline, where flower-clad cliffs tower over beautiful bays. 22 miles (35km) driving, whole day tour

Allow a whole day for all the diversions, take a picnic lunch or stop for a bite of freshly caught seafood. The pretty bay of **Bonne Nuit**, with a beach, car park and excellent café, makes an ideal place for a break.

The majestic cliffs of the north extend along the entire coast, affording spectacular views across to the other Channel Islands and France.

Dotting the shore are half a dozen little bays, with fishing ports sheltered by rocky headlands. Each of these links up with the north coast footpath, which runs all the way from **Rozel** in the east to **Grosnez** in the west.

Try to cover at least a small section of this glorious coastline on foot. Choose a clear day so you can enjoy the views – and preferably when

there's not a north or easterly wind. Don't forget to bring binoculars for spotting the birds that have habitats in the crevices and rocky outcrops. Species you are likely to see are fulmars, cormorants and shags, and – if you happen to be at Plémont in the spring, you might spy a puffin. Dolphins, grey seals and basking sharks are also occasionally seen from the cliff paths.

Stop for a crab sandwich at the Hungry Man kiosk in Rozel Bay.

ROZEL

From the St Helier ring road follow signs for 'The North' and the Five Oaks roundabout. From here take the A6 to St Martin's, then follow the B38 up to **Rozel Bay ❶**.

Tucked away in the northeast corner of the island, this is a small, picturesque creek where fishermen's houses overlook the tiny harbour and the sand and shingle beach. The pier was built in 1829, during the heyday of the oyster industry, when there were around 30 oyster fishing vessels based in the small port. Beside the pier you're unlikely to miss the legendary Hungry Man kiosk, famous for its fabulous crab sandwiches.

Being the closest point in Jersey to France, at the height of the Napoleonic threat Rozel was considered a valuable defence site. However, no shot was ever fired here in battle.

The lush **Rozel Valley**, tucked away behind the village, makes a pleasant inland walk with its exotic trees and shrubs. Subtropical flora were first planted here by a 19th-century naturalist, Samuel Curtis, and some of them can still be seen today. The Château la Chaire hotel has a lovely valley setting and offers fine dining in an oak-panelled restaurant or lighter fare and afternoon tea in the conservatory brasserie.

BOULEY BAY

Head westwards out of Rozel on the C93 and after 1.2 miles (2km) turn right into the Rue du Bouillons (C95). At the next junction turn right and from here follow signs for **Bouley Bay ❷**. As you near the coast the road snakes its way down through the wooded hillside to a pebble bay surrounded by high cliffs. The steeply shelving beach and the deepest waters around the island's shores are ideal for scuba-diving or snorkelling. The sea here is rich in marine life, including lobsters, crabs, sea urchins and starfish, along with many species of fish.

Wander off the beaten track into St Catherine's Wood, otherwise known as Rozel Woods.

Bouley Bay and the fort of
L'Etacquerel.

The **Bouley Bay Dive Centre,**
based below the Water's Edge Cha-
lets, offers lessons and facilities to
divers of all standards, including 'try
dives' for complete beginners. Bouley Bay is also the venue of the very
popular Hillclimbs, which take place
up the steep and twisty road from the
bay four times a year.

Any member of the Jersey Motor
Cycle and Light Car Club equipped
with motorbike, saloon car, racing car,
sports car or even a bike is welcome
to participate. The village is otherwise
peaceful, with no more to it than the
hotel, a café above the beach and the
Black Dog Pub, named after the fic-
titious **Black Dog of Bouley Bay**
(see box).

Fort L'Etacquerel and Fort Leicester

On the east side of the bay, perched
above the sea, the fort of **L'Etacquerel ❸** was one of several defences built to guard the north coast
from French invaders. Another was
Fort Leicester to the west of the
bay, reached up the steps to the left
just before the jetty. Both forts have
been converted into holiday accommodation by Jersey Heritage, L'Etacquerel providing 'stone tent' accommodation for 30 with sleeping bags,
Fort Leicester a relatively comfortable
sea-view retreat for up to eight people. Cliff paths either side of Bouley
Bay provide delightful walks. In summer the hills are ablaze with heather
and wild flowers, while shags, which

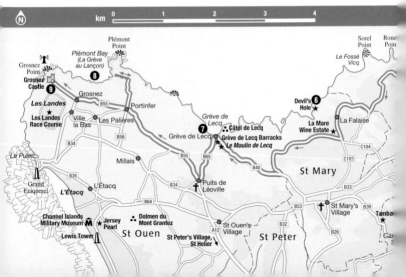

The Black Dog of Bouley Bay.

nest in cliff crevices in the spring, can be seen flying close to the shore.

BONNE NUIT

Leaving Bouley Bay, climb back up to the top of the hill and turn right at the T-junction along the Rue de la Petite Falaise (C96). In less than half a mile turn right to join the main A8. Take the next main right turn (B63) and follow the signs for Bonne Nuit.

To the right **Les Platons**, at 420ft (133 metres) above sea level, is the highest spot in Jersey – hence the forest of TV and radio masts. The deep cave at **Belle Hougue Point**, where the remains of prehistoric deer were

Black Dog of Bouley Bay

During the latter half of the 18th century numerous tales were told of the Black Dog of Bouley Bay, a huge beast which roamed the cliffs around the bay, dragging its chain behind it. The dog would terrify victims by circling them with the chain, leaving them unharmed but in a state of shock. Any rumour of the Black Dog roaming the region and the locals would hot-foot it home. The stories are believed to have been the invention of smugglers – of whom there were many at the time – to frighten prying parishioners away from the bay and leave the coast clear to land their cargoes of spirits and tobacco.

discovered, lies below. Only experienced climbers, with ropes, should contemplate attempting the descent.

The name **Bonne Nuit** ❹ (Good Night) appears to have derived from the now non-existent Chapel of Bona Nochte, built in the 12th century. Conversely, the sea beyond the bay used to be called

Secluded Bonne Nuit Bay was a prime spot for smuggling in the 17th and 18th centuries; its pier is now the finishing point for an annual rowing race.

Maurepos (Bad Repose), possibly on account of smugglers.

Today it is a secluded little bay, with a tiny harbour and a sand and shingle beach, sheltered below heather-clad hills. At low tide fishing boats and pleasure cruisers are beached on the sands, and resident mallard ducks waddle across the bay, hoping for a crust or two from the Bonne Nuit Beach Café (see page 81).

The red wooden huts on the jetty belong to fishermen who go out daily for lobsters, crabs and clams. In ancient times fishermen and other islanders rowed around Le Cheval Guillaume or Cheval Roc, the offshore rock, to protect them from evil spirits. Bonne Nuit pier is the finishing point for the Sark to Jersey Rowing Race, held either in June or July depending on the tides, and a plaque, unveiled by

Sorel Point

As you head northwest you will see a sign to Sorel Point, which is the most northerly tip of the island, commanding magnificent sea views. Weather permitting, you can make out the islands of Alderney, Guernsey, Sark, the coast of Normandy and the Paternoster Reef closer to shore. Keep your eyes focused out to sea and make sure to avoid the views to the east – Ronez Quarry is one of the very few blots on the north coast landscape.

Solitary Sorel Point.

The soft wool of the Manx Loagthan sheep is prized by weavers.

Chay Blyth (who, with John Ridgeway, rowed the Atlantic in 92 days in 1966) commemorates the silver jubilee. The fastest rowers from Sark take about 2.5 hours.

LA CRÊTE FORT

On the promontory to the east of the bay **La Crête Fort** ❺ was built by the British in 1835, on a site that was first militarised in the 16th century. The fort was extended during the German Occupation in World War II, and until a few years ago was used by the Lieutenant-Governor as a weekend retreat. Jersey Heritage has renovated the fort for holiday lets. Tenants can enjoy spectacular sea views to Guernsey, Sark and France, and there's a secluded beach close by.

Take the C99 out of Bonne Nuit, going westwards and when you arrive at the T-junction turn right on to the B52. This will take you to the village of St John's where you turn right on to the main A9. After the church take another right turn, on to the C101, which merges into the C100.

Resident mallard ducks patrol the beach at Bonne Nuit Bay.

DEVIL'S HOLE

The main road veers away from the coast and becomes a Green Lane (with a speed limit of 15mph/24k-mh). At the next crossroads turn right for Le Creux du Vis (Screw Hole) or, as it is more popularly known, **Devil's Hole** ❻. Park at the Priory Inn and take the steep footpath down the hill to see this spectacular natural feature, a great blowhole, created by a collapsed cave.

The melodramatic name is thought to have derived from the figurehead of a mid-19th-century French shipwreck, which was washed up in the Devil's Hole and crafted into a wooden horned devil. Over the years various replicas of the devil have been placed on the path going down to add atmosphere, but each one has been stolen. The latest one is made of metal and dominates the pond at the start of the path near the pub.

The land is owned by the Jersey National Trust, which was responsible for the work carried out at the site to provide safer access for visitors.

The sea flows into the spectacular Devil's Hole.

Wooden steps have been replaced by a tarmac path with handrails leading to a viewing platform, telescope and interpretation panels, and a further decked platform offers sight of the Devil's Hole and the waters crashing as the tide comes up.

Cliffs and rocky headlands protect the intimate, sandy beach at Grève de Lecq – the north coast's most popular and busiest family beach.

La Mare Wine Estate

Going south from Devil's Hole, you may want to check out all the Jersey specialities at La Mare Wine Estate (see page 62). You're unlikely to have time for a guided tour and tasting of the winery, but you can get access to the shop (and café) without having to pay the admission fee.

The shop has a tempting selection of sparkling and still wines, liqueurs, chocolates and a whole range of preserves – all made at La Mare.

Chocolate heaven at La Mare Wine Estate gift shop.

GRÈVE DE LECQ

From Devil's Hole follow the road south towards the village of St Mary, and take the signs for Grève de Lecq. In the 1860s a decision was made to create a safe harbour for boats from the island's large fishing fleet. But this never came about. The original pier, started in 1872, was poorly constructed and almost entirely demolished by storms. It lay in ruins for years, and it was not until the following century that it was finally made safe – as a truncated little jetty.

Today **Grève de Lecq ❼** is a popular beach resort, drawing far more visitors than any of the other north coast bays. It offers ample parking, easy access, a sandy beach and a couple of cafés. Children and ducks enjoy the sands here and fishermen cast their lines from the jetty. Overlooking the bay to the east and reached along the coastal path, **Le Câtel de Lecq** (Lecq Castle) is

The old pier at Grève de Lecq is an excellent vantage point for budding young anglers.

Behind the beach, the National Trust for Jersey has restored the Grève de Lecq barracks from the Napoleonic Wars.

said to have been the site of an Iron Age hill fort.

Grève de Lecq Barracks

Standing behind the bay, the **Grève de Lecq Barracks** (May–Sept Wed Sun 11am–4pm) were built to house garrison troops in 1810 when the island feared a French invasion. Re-stored by the National Trust, the barracks are today home to the North Coast Visitors' Centre, devoted to the wildlife and history of the area, plus history and military exhibits and a collection of horse-drawn carriages. The officers' quarters at the Barracks have been converted into holiday lets.

Le Moulin de Lecq

Further back along the main road, **Le Moulin de Lecq**, which has been converted into an inn, was formerly a flour-grinding watermill. It dates from the 14th century, was used for over 600 years and still retains its massive mill wheel. The stream here, which gushes out on to the beach, is the dividing line between the parishes of St Mary and St Ouen.

PLÉMONT

The last beach on the north coast is **Plémont ❽**, or more correctly La Grève au Lançon (Sand-Eel Beach). To get there, take the road out of Grève de Lecq (the B65), turning right on to the B55, and right again at the small crossroads at Portinfer. Plémont beach to the north remains unspoilt thanks largely to the lack of vehicular access.

Refreshments await you at Le Moulin de Lecq inn.

welcome

REAL ALES
GOOD FOOD

Jersey Puffins

Atlantic puffins inhabit the northwest corner of Jersey nesting in the cliffs from Plémont east to Grand Becquet. Puffins lay only one egg per year, and the decline in numbers is of great concern. The causes of the decline are not clear, but disturbance by humans may well be a factor. Hence a seabird protection zone has been established here to try to enhance breeding success.

Leave the car at the park above the bay and walk down the cliff path then take the long flight of steps that leads from the café down to the beach. Low tide reveals a wide expanse of fine sands, rock pools and a network of caves in the cliffs on the landward side; but at high tide there is no sand to be seen. The headland to the east, accessible by the north coast footpath, is a good place for birdwatching, especially in late spring/summer. The cliffs here have been home to a colony of puffins for over 100 years (see box).

In 2015 Jersey residents heaved a sigh of relief when it was announced that the beautiful headland above Plémont Bay would be restored to its natural state. For years the site of a derelict Pontins holiday camp, it was purchased by a commercial company who threatened to build a large development here. The National Trust successfully campaigned against the project and after a hearing in Jersey's Royal Court, and with help from the States of Jersey, the park was sold to the trust in a multi-million deal. The campsite has been demolished and archaeologists are now examining the area.

LES LANDES

Returning to Portinfer, rejoin the B55 going westwards. Take the next turning to the right, a narrow road signed to **Les Landes Race Course**, which lies to the left as you head towards the cliffs.

Race meetings have been taking place on the island for over 170 years. The first races in the 1830s were held on the flat sands

Le Moulin de Lecq, now a public house, was one of the many ancient watermills of the island.

Walk This Way

The north coast footpath offers mile after mile of majestic cliffs and dramatic rugged scenery. This is easily the most exhilarating walk on the island, and one that can either be done in its entirety over a very long day (roughly eight hours) or preferably in separate sections at a gentler pace. The walk can be done at any time of year, but the scenery is at its best in spring, when sea campion, thrift, ox-eye daisies, pennywort and bluebells are in full bloom. This is also the time of year that you might spot the Glanville fritillary butterfly dancing over the cliffs.

Wild foxgloves are a common sight on the north coast footpath.

of St Aubin's beach, then at Greve d'Azette (St Helier), where several thousand spectators used to watch the big events. Gorey Common hosted the races for over 60 years, and special boats used to come from Guernsey for the events. Lillie Langtry, who later bred her own horses,

The deserted coast at Plémont.

was one of the famous visitors here. Les Landes is a spectacularly located course, but race meetings these days are point-to-point style, without the glamour of bygone days.

GROSNEZ CASTLE

At the end of the road, at the most northwesterly point of the island, stand the evocative medieval ruins of the **Castle of Grosnez** ❾. The only recognisable feature is the Gothic arch, although the foundations of walls and buildings beyond it are clearly visible.

A reconstruction on the information panel shows how the castle would have originally looked, complete with drawbridge, portcullis and machicolated upper storey. Unlike Jersey's other main strongholds, little is known of the castle's history.

It was a roughly built fort, constructed in the first half of the 14th century

A lap of honour for a jockey and his horse at Les Landes Race Course, next to the ruins of Grosnez Castle.

in defence against an invasion from the French, then destroyed, probably by the French, either in the same century, or when they occupied Jersey in 1461–8. The carved corbels that

The main gateway, bastions and a narrow moat are all that remain of Grosnez Castle.

once decorated the main arch fell off long ago, but were rescued and safely housed in the Archaeological Museum at La Hougue Bie (see page 85). The ruins are set dramatically on the clifftops, 200ft (60 metres) above the rough seas. Walk through the arch for fine views, weather permitting, of all the other Channel Islands.

Looking from left to right these are Guernsey, Jethou, Herm, Sark and in the very far distance, Alderney. The coast of Normandy lies in the distance to the east, while closer inland, a chain of uninhabitable rocks known as **Pater Noster** (Our Father) is visible at low tide.

The name originated from a shipwreck here, involving families who were on their way to colonise the then uninhabited island of Sark. Several of them were drowned, including women and children.

Since then it has been customary for sailors and fishermen to recite the Lord's Prayer as they pass the treacherous reef.

Walking the north coast footpath is an exhilarating experience.

NORTH COAST FOOTPATH

The official **north coast footpath** runs for 15 miles (24km) almost the entire length of the coast. Parts of the walk are quite steep, particularly

A stone signpost points the way on the north coast footpath.

as the path climbs up from the bays, but it can be exhilarating, and there is nothing that would really challenge an averagely fit adult. The path occasionally breaks from the coast, diverting through wooded slopes or fields, and in St John's Parish, it joins the main road, following the coast, before heading inland to avoid the unsightly quarry at Ronez.

The public bus service provides the best means of transport – whether you're doing the whole walk or different sections on different days. Services from St Helier operate to points on or close to the north coast, and it's easy to hop off and on.

Bus timetables are available from Visit Jersey, Liberation Bus Station or www.libertybus.je. If you have your own car, leave it at one of the bays and take a bus back to the parking place.

Although the footpath is well signed and fairly obvious, a map is nevertheless useful. The best one is the Ordnance Survey style Jersey Official Leisure map, available from Visit Jersey or from bookshops.

Take time to admire the flora on your coastal walk.

Eating Out

Rozel Bay
Château la Chaire Restaurant
Rozel; tel: 01534-863 354; www.
chateau-la-chaire.co.uk; lunch and
dinner Wed–Mon.
Behind the bay, in the wooded Rozel
valley, this inviting country house
hotel offers excellent English cooking
with a Gallic influence, in a delightful
dining room or in the conservatory
with terrace in summer. £££
The Rozel
La Vallée de Rozel; tel: 01534-863 438;
www.rozelpubanddining.co.uk; lunch
and dinner Mon–Sat, lunch on Sun.
Newly-furnished inn with stone and
wood floors, real ales and bar billiards.
Meals served in the modern upstairs
restaurant are definitely a cut above
your average pub and the emphasis is
on locally-caught fish and seafood. ££

Bouley Bay
Mad Mary's
Bouley Bay Beach, Trinity; Apr–Oct
daily 9.30am–5pm.
Lovely sea-view terrace where
you can enjoy crab sandwiches,
home-made cakes, bacon butties,
cream teas and Mary's legendary
hot chocolate with cream and
marshmallows. £

Bonne Nuit
Bonne Nuit Beach Café
Bonne Nuit Beach; tel: 01534-861
656; www.bonnenuitbeachcafe.co.uk;
daily 8.30am–9pm

One of the north coast's most popular
cafés, looking on to the lovely Bonne
Nuit Bay and serving everything from
all day breakfasts (Apr–Oct) to seafood,
salads and afternoon tea, plus Thai
specials. The café is not licensed so
bring your own bottle. £–££

St John
Les Fontaines
La Route du Nord; tel: 01534-862
707; daily noon–2.15pm, 6–8.30pm
(Sun until 8pm).
Charming country pub on the north
coast road close to Sorel Point,
converted from a farmhouse with a
pleasant sea-view terrace and first-
class pub food. Indoor and outdoor
play areas. £–££

Grève de Lecq
Le Moulin de Lecq
Le Mont de la Grève de Lecq; tel:
01534-482 818; www.moulindelecq.
com; daily 11am–11pm, food served
noon–2pm, 6–9pm.
This 14th-century inn has a
characterful bar and a restaurant
serving full meals. There's also a
working water mill and garden with
adventure playground. ££

Plémont
Plémont Beach Café
Tel: 01534-482 005; daily 9am–5pm.
This café above Plémont Beach
prides itself on supporting local food
and art, which is reflected in both the
menu and the decor. £

Hall of Fame

For a tiny island, Jersey can boast some big names, from painters, poets and novelists to golfers and racing drivers, the most celebrated being the actress Lillie Langtry

The 19th century saw political exiles and literati, lured by the coastal scenery and healthy climate, while in more recent times running from the Inland Revenue has been the main reason for celebrities to settle here.

LILLIE LANGTRY 1853–1929

"She has no right to be intelligent, daring and independent as well as lovely." (George Bernard Shaw)

The only daughter of a philandering Rector of St Saviour and Dean of Jersey, Emilie Charlotte Le Breton was born in the parish of St Saviour in 1853. At the age of 21 she married a wealthy widower, Edward Langtry, and two years later took London society by storm with her beauty, vivacity and charm. Among her many famous admirers were Oscar Wilde, who once referred to her as "the second Helen of Troy", President Roosevelt "She's so pretty she takes away man's breath", and artists such as James Whistler and Jersey-born John Everett Millais. But the most famous admirer was the Prince of Wales, later to become Edward VII, a renowned womaniser who took "the Jersey Lily" as his semi-official mistress. Many years later she caused further furore by

Lillie Langtry in all her glory.

Anthony Trollope (1815–82). The English novelist worked for the postal service for over 30 years, visited Jersey to research the delivery of mail and introduced the pillar box in St Helier in 1854 – the first in the British Isles.

George Eliot (1819–80). The novelist came to Jersey in 1857 with her lover, George Lewes, and was disowned by her family.

John Everett Millais (1829–96), a founder member of the Pre-Raphaelite brotherhood. He later became a fashionable painter of portraits and genre pieces. His famous painting of Lillie Langtry, *A Jersey Lily*, can be seen in the Jersey Museum.

Karl Marx and **Friedrich Engels**, founders of modern socialism, made several visits to Jersey between 1857 and 1885. This was probably for health reasons as they were hardly polite about the island, or its visitors.

Harry Vardon (1870–1937). Professional golfer. Winner of the American Open, the German Open and six times winner of the British Open. He was born in Grouville, Jersey.

Gerald Durrell (1925–95). Celebrated author and naturalist, who set up Jersey Zoo (now the Durrell Wildlife Conservation Trust) in 1959.

Jack Higgins (b.1929, real name Harry Patterson). Author of over 60 novels, including *The Fox*, set in Jersey during the Occupation, and *The Eagle has Landed*. Lives in Jersey.

Nigel Mansell (b.1953). Former British racing driver who won the Formula One World Championship in 1992. Mansell moved to Jersey in 1997 and has a mansion at St Brelade's Bay. His motoring memorabilia, with video footage, trophies and racing cars, can be viewed at The Mansell Collection (www.themansellcollection.co.uk).

becoming the first society woman to take to the stage. Lillie toured the US and South Africa as an actress, became a racehorse owner, and spent her last years in Monaco, where she died at the age of 75. She is buried in the graveyard of St Saviour's Church, next to the rectory where she was born.

JERSEY CONNECTIONS

Sir Walter Raleigh (1552–1618). Governor of Jersey, who named Elizabeth Castle after his revered queen.

Victor Hugo (1802–85). Novelist, poet and dramatist who lived in Jersey from 1852–55 (see page 98).

Mont Orgueil, Jersey's oldest castle.

Tour 6

Sights of the East

History, gastronomy, gardens and beaches – the southeast has it all, and this exciting 18-mile (30km) whole-day driving tour caters for all tastes

Mont Orgueil Castle, set spectacularly above Gorey harbour and commanding the entire east coast, is the most photographed landmark on the island. The medieval fortress played a major role in Jersey's tempestuous history, repulsing repeated French invasions from 1204–1600. The quaint harbour below Mont Orgueil Castle and the spacious sands of the Royal Bay of Grouville provide a pleasant break from sightseeing, while the gardens of Samarès Manor are the highlight of the return trip to town.

A legacy of more ancient history is La Hougue Bie, a finely preserved Neolithic passage grave, its mound a dominant feature of the landscape for 6,000 years.

Highlights

- La Hougue Bie
- Mont Orgueil Castle
- Gorey Harbour
- Royal Bay of Grouville
- Samarès Manor

Take the St Helier ring road, following signs first for the north and then for the A7 to the Five Oaks roundabout. This will take you through the parish of St Saviour, where actress Lillie Langtry (see page 82), was born. She was married twice in the **Church of St Saviour**, and is buried in the churchyard here. Government House, south of the church, is the official residence of the Lieutenant-Governor, the Queen's representative on the island.

LA HOUGUE BIE

At the Five Oaks roundabout, turn right on to Princes Tower Road (the B28). From here follow the signs for **La Hougue Bie** ❶ (www.jerseyheritage. org; late Mar–Oct daily 10am–5pm, mid Feb to late Mar, Sun 10am-4pm). This remarkable site, in the heart of the countryside, is dominated by a burial mound, covering a Neolithic passage grave, dating from about 3500 BC. The word "Hougue" derives from the Norse *haugre*, meaning a burial mound, and the "Bie" was probably a corruption of the Norman family name of Hambye.

The site can be a bit confusing, and it's worth watching the short film presentation near the entrance before you start your visit.

This intriguing site abounds with legends, and notably the tales of the dragon which lived in the marshes of St Lawrence and terrified the islanders. Hearing of their plight, the gallant Seigneur of Hambye came from his castle in Normandy and slew the dragon. After the long battle he fell asleep and his squire, who had designs on his master's wife, murdered him and buried the body.

The squire returned to Hambye, leading the wife to believe that the dragon had killed her husband and

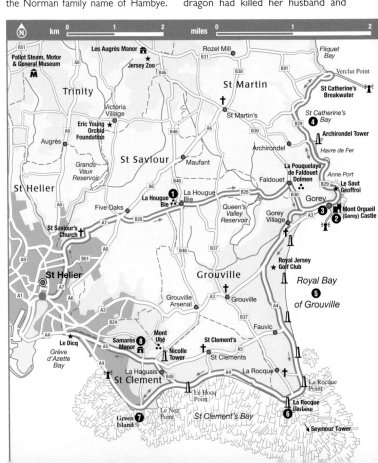

La Hougue Bie is one of the largest and best-preserved passage graves in Europe and dates back to 3500 BC.

he (the squire) had gallantly slain the dragon. The Seigneur's dying wish, he told her, was for his wife to marry the servant who had avenged his death. She agreed to marry the squire but the new Lord Hambye soon disclosed his guilt in his sleep. On discovering the truth Lady Hambye came to Jersey and buried her husband under a mound (La Hougue Bie) on the site of his grave. She ordered the mound to be built so high she could spy it from her castle keep in France. The mound was named La Hougue Hambye.

History of La Hougue Bie

Excavations under the mound in 1924 revealed a low passage leading to chambers made of huge stone blocks. The mound is 40ft (12 metres) high and covers a chamber that is 33ft (10 metres) long. The larger stone slabs may have been dragged from a distance of 4 miles (6km), possibly on sledges or rollers. Fragments of bone from eight bodies, along with flint tools, bones of sheep, pig and ox, beads and pottery were all discovered

within the dolmen. Limpet shells were also found here, proving that way back in prehistoric times the farmers were enjoying Jersey seafood.

The old pagan site had been Christianised by the construction of two medieval chapels on top of the mound. The first was Notre Dame de la Clarté, dating from the

Inside the chapel of Notre Dame de la Clarté at La Hougue Bie.

Inside the geology and archaeology museum at La Hougue Bie are fine examples of flint tools found at La Cotte de St Brelade.

12th century, but heavily restored. Four centuries later the local dean rebuilt its chancel, which became known as the **Jerusalem Chapel**. During the Reformation the chapels were abandoned, but in the late 18th century were transformed by Philippe d'Auvergne, Duke of Bouillon, a scholar and eminent sea captain. Straddling the two chapels he built **The Prince's Tower** (La Tour d'Auvergne as it was known), a neo-Gothic folly which became one of the most distinctive and dramatic landmarks of the island. In the early 19th century the tower became one of Jersey's first tourist attractions, offering panoramic views. In the late 1830s it was extended to create the Prince's Tower Hotel, which became popular for eating, drinking and dancing. But by the late 19th century the tower was derelict. A restoration committee in 1924 de-

Dean Mabon's Miracles

Richard Mabon, Dean of Jersey from 1509, built a small oratory under the Jerusalem Chapel, which was inspired by his pilgrimage to the Holy Sepulchre in Jerusalem. Mabon claimed to receive visions of the Virgin Mary while he was praying in the crypt and organised for pilgrims to visit the site. According to a Protestant chronicler, the Dean used to fake miracles here, making money from gullible pilgrims.

Two chapels under one roof at La Hougue Bie.

cided – against the wishes of most of the islanders – that the Prince's Tower be demolished so that the medieval chapels could be restored to their original form.

Visiting La Hougue Bie

To access the burial chamber below the mound you have to stoop right down and walk along the dark, tunnel-like passage grave. The mysterious chamber, together with the side chambers, is likely to have served not only for burials but as a ritual and ceremonial site (not that there's much space for festivities). From the bottom of the mound a spiral path winds up to the chapels on the top. Switch on the lights in the Jerusalem Chapel to see the traces of two archangels on the wall.

At ground level you can visit the geology and archaeology museum, which displays bones and teeth of prehistoric animals discovered at La Cotte de St Brelade (see page 41). A legacy of more recent history is the German command bunker at the foot

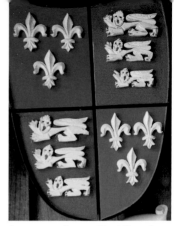

Jersey coat of arm at Mont Orgueil Castle.

of the mound, housing a poignant exhibition dedicated to slave workers in the Channel Islands. The Germans also constructed a watchtower on top of the mound at the west end (no longer extant) and 70 trenches within the grounds.

MONT ORGUEIL CASTLE

Turn right out of La Hougue Bie and follow the signs for **Gorey** on

Built on the site of an Iron Age hill fort, Mont Orgueil Castle stood up to several full-scale attacks between the 13th and 15th centuries.

Taking in the views from the castle battlements.

Somerset Tower

A climb up the steep castle battlements to Somerset Tower will reward you with a jaw-dropping panorama. You can see why the Germans adapted the tower as an observation post in World War II. France can usually be seen across the water, and on a really clear day you can make out the power station at Cap de la Hague on the tip of the Cherbourg peninsula.

the east coast. Nearing the village, a steep road brings you down to that most famous of Jersey landmarks, **Mont Orgueil Castle** ❷ (www.jerseyheritage.org; Apr–Oct daily 10am–6pm, Nov–Mar Fri–Mon 10am–4pm). Translated as Mount Pride, and also known as Gorey Castle, this mighty fortress towers over the harbour and commands spectacular views. A fine example of a concentric castle, it was sited on an Iron Age hill fort and designed with a series of independent defences, with walls going straight out of the rock.

The castle is an impressive site at any time of day, but particularly picturesque after dark in summer when the battlements are floodlit.

Impregnable fortress

From 1204, when King John lost the English territories in France and the Channel Islands elected to remain loyal to the English crown, hostilities prevailed between the islands and France. Jersey was frequently threatened by invasions, and fortifications were constructed, particularly along the vulnerable east coast, lying just 14 miles (22km) from Normandy.

Mont Orgueil was built on a promontory overlooking the French

coast and remained the main stronghold on the island for nearly four centuries. The great medieval fortress withstood many attacks from the French, including a devastating raid in 1373 by the Constable of France, Bertrand du Guesclin, otherwise known as the Black Dog of Brittany. During its long history, the castle fell just once, in 1461, and a French force captured and held the island for the next seven years. Although the castle had been adapted to accommodate cannon, and later

Detail of an equestrian statue in the castle grounds.

Children can raid the dressing-up box at Mont Orgueil Castle, and spend their visit transformed into a medieval queen or a knight in shining armour.

transformed into an artillery fortress, it could not keep up with the demands of modern-day warfare.

In the late 16th century the decision was taken to build a new fortress, Elizabeth Castle, in St Aubin's Bay. Mont Orgueil became redundant and known as *Le Vieux Château*. Were it not for the intervention of Sir Walter Raleigh, who thought it a shame to lose such a "stately fort", the castle would have been razed to the ground.

In the 17th and 18th centuries the castle played various roles: a stronghold of the Royalists in the English Civil War, a state prison under Cromwell, an island prison for those identified as witches, a refuge for French aristocrats and the headquarters of a spy network during the French Revolution. You can still see the chamber where William Prynne, the 17th-century puritan, began his sentence. Not only incarcerated, he had his ears cut off and the initials S.L. (Seditious Libeller) branded upon his cheek. In 1907 the castle was given to the people of Jersey

Birds are trained using techniques dating from the Middle Ages.

Living History

May to October a series of events from Jersey Heritage bring to life the island's history through costumed interpretations, set against the backdrop of historic sites. At Mont Orgueil Castle see medieval swordsmen practising their skills, or perhaps enjoy music and juggling performed by the court jesters, or watch a demonstration of medieval falconry. See www.jerseyheritage.org for a list of what's on.

One of many sculptures inside the castle.

by the crown for use as a historic monument and visitor attraction. In 1940 the Germans fortified the site with observation towers, trenches and gun emplacements, and the keep was used as a barracks.

Climbing the ramparts

It's a long haul to the top, via cobbled passages, paths and stairways, with fine views all the way. En route you can explore towers, batteries, cellars, chapels, medieval halls – and more. A series of stand-alone exhibits are scattered throughout the castle, all providing a flavour of the medieval era and Jersey's role within it. These are mostly sculptures, many of them very striking, ranging from replica Tudor artillery pieces and life-size figures manning the ramparts to witches and warriors, a urine wheel (used by medieval physicians to diagnose patients by the colour of their urine) and the gory *Wound Man*, pierced by spears and daggers. Keeping history alive, there are experts demonstrating Tudor hawking and military weapons, medieval singers, a room of dressing up

clothes and wooden soldiers with bows and arrows at the ready.

GOREY HARBOUR

In the shadow of the castle lies the quaint harbour of **Gorey** ❸, where shops, pubs and cafés cluster around the waterfront. The quayside offers plenty of places to stop for a bite, among them Feast, see page 99.

The original village expanded in the late 18th and early 19th centuries when the flourishing oyster industry gave Gorey the sobriquet of "the pearl of the east". Oysters were discovered on the muddy seabed between Jersey and Normandy in 1797. The catches were exported to England in large quantities and the trade flourished. Following the decline of the oyster fishing trade

A view of the castle gardens and Gorey harbour.

Jersey oysters are cultivated on the rugged east coast near La Rocque.

at Whitstable, hundreds of English oyster fishermen invaded the coast to share in the profits. By the 1830s the village had doubled in size; there were 250 oyster fishing ships, bringing in around 12,000 oysters on each trip. By the middle of the century the oyster beds had been over-fished and the industry was all but over. You can still find a few oysters on the rocks, but those on your plate will have been nurtured in farms in Grouville Bay. Over 4 million oysters are now produced annually.

St Helier to Paris

By 1881 you could buy a through ticket all the way from St Helier to Paris. You travelled with the Jersey Eastern Railway Company to Gorey station, by horse and cart to Gorey pier, then a steamer across to Carteret and from here on the new railway line to Paris. However, the company suffered competition from buses, introduced in Jersey in the 1920s, and in 1929 it went into liquidation.

Gorey harbour today protects a fleet of pleasure craft and, as the only official seaport in Jersey apart from St Helier, offers high-speed catamaran trips to the port of Carteret in Normandy. If you decide on a trip, don't forget you will need your passport.

ST CATHERINE'S BAY

From Gorey, follow the coastal B29 north. The road skirts the pebble and sandy bay of Anne Port, and follows the coast by the bay of Havre de Fer and past the distinctive red-and-white **Archirondel Tower**, built in 1874. The tower has recently been restored and can now be hired for basic holiday lets through Jersey Heritage. Keep to the B29 for **St Catherine's Bay ❶**, enclosed to the north by a 0.6-mile (1km) -long breakwater which was built as a result of a British blunder in the mid-19th century.

In answer to a naval base at Cherbourg and other French coastal installations, the British Government chose this site (as well as one at Alderney) for a harbour. Despite warnings that the depth of water was insufficient and the harbour would silt up, the project neverthe-

The Archirondel Tower at St Catherine's Bay.

Geoffrey's Leap

North of Gorey the coast road climbs up towards the rocky promontory known as Le Saut Geoffroi or Geoffrey's Leap, named after a convicted criminal and renowned womaniser who managed to survive unscathed after his punishment of jumping from the cliffs to the rocks below. He was declared a freed man but, eager to impress the fair sex, he decided to perform the feat again. This time, however, his luck ran out.

less went ahead and a breakwater was built here, with another one started at Archirondel. Twenty years and £250,000 later, the project was abandoned. The St Catherine's arm of the harbour was preserved and a lighthouse built at the end.

Today the breakwater is a popular spot for fishing and promenading, and the Breakwater Café offers good views from its outdoor tables, see page 99.

Just south of the breakwater, a German bunker houses tanks of around 6,500 turbot, ranging from tiddlers to mature 2.5lb (1kg) fish. The large ones are sold to restaurateurs, fishmongers and the public. In summer there are guided tours on request (24-hr notice, tel: 01534-868 836; www.jersey.com/jersey-turbot).

The coast road stops at this northern end of St Catherine's Bay, but you can get to Fliquet Bay to the north on foot.

ROYAL BAY OF GROUVILLE

East of Gorey Village, the **Royal Bay of Grouville** ❺ stretches for 3 miles (5km) between Gorey and La Rocque Point. Guarding the bay are

a number of towers built as coastal defences in the second half of the 18th century. These fortifications were armed and manned, but never actually used to defend the island. Some of them have now been converted to private residences. Queen Victoria, so impressed by this long and spacious sandy bay, gave it the Royal prefix after her visit in 1859.

Beach fun on the Royal Bay of Grouville.

Moon Walk

For a unique experience take a "moonwalk" on the seabed to Seymour Tower. Through guided walks organised by Jersey Walk Adventures (www.jerseywalkadventures.co.uk) you can explore the savage low-tide seascape of gutters, reefs, tidal flats, lagoons, sandbanks and boulder fields – said to resemble the surface of the moon. During night walks the tiny creatures in the water and the seaweed glow in the dark like fireflies or glow worms. Prepare to get your feet wet!

Enjoy a hike across the lunar seascape.

Today the beach is popular with sunbathers and water sports enthusiasts. Gorey Water Sports (www.goreywatersports.co.uk) offer a range of aquatic activities in summer from wakeboarding and water skiing to banana and sofa rides. As you go south you'll see the links of the **Royal Jersey Golf Club**, the most exclusive on the island. Harry Vardon, six times British Open Championship winner, was born in Grouville.

SEYMOUR TOWER

The route returns to St Helier via the coast road, the A4, stopping at the little harbour of **La Rocque ❻** on the southeastern tip of the island. It was here that Baron de Rullecourt and his troops secretly landed in January 1781,

The isolated Seymour Tower was built as part of Jersey's coastal defence and dates back to the 18th century.

A statue of Harry Vardon, six times Open golf champion, takes a swing at the Royal Jersey Golf Club.

en route to their defeat at Royal Square in St Helier (see page 20). Low tide reveals a vast lunar landscape of reefs, gullies and rock pools (see page 96). Seymour Tower, standing on a rocky islet 2 miles (3km) to the southeast, has stood guard over the island since 1782. It can be reached on foot, but beware of the large tidal flow and the rapid incoming waters: the sea can rise

18ins (50cm) in 10 minutes. (Check the times of the tides in the *Jersey Post* or at www.gov.je, inserting 'Tide times' in the search box). For the adventurous there is the opportunity of staying at the tower overnight. Access is restricted to specific days, dependent on the tides, and all groups must be accompanied by an accredited guide (for further information visit www.jerseyheritage.org).

Green Island is only an island at high tide.

GREEN ISLAND

From La Rocque continue on the A4, detouring briefly after 2.5 miles (4km) at **Green Island ❼**, a few hundred metres off the coast and the most southerly in the British Isles. A small rocky outcrop covered in grass (hence the name), it is only an island when the tide is high and is otherwise accessible by foot. Prehistoric graves, along with human and animal bones, were discovered here in 1911, but were removed for safekeeping to the Jersey Museum in St Helier. The island has gradually been eroded by the sea, and restorers are currently trying to prevent it from being washed away.

The main attraction here is the **Green Island Restaurant**,

Samarès Manor is an elegant house set in extensive grounds incorporating ornamental gardens and ponds with swans.

perched at the top of the slope and offering amazing views from the terrace, which is the perfect sun-trap in summer (see page 99).

RAMSAR SITE

This southeastern corner of Jersey, equating to 25 percent of the

The Herb Garden at Samarès has a unique collection of culinary and medicinal plants.

island's landmass, is designated as a Ramsar Site. In 1971 34 countries signed the Convention on Wetlands of International Importance, drawing attention to threatened wetlands. The Convention was adopted at Ramsar, the Iranian town on the southern shores of the Caspian Sea – hence the name of threatened sites. The low-lying south and southeast coast are also prime areas for ornithologists. The vast expanse of mud, sand and rocky outcrops provides a rich breeding ground for thousands of wintering waders, gulls and wildfowl. Plovers, redshank, turnstone, dunlin, bar-tailed godwits, curlew and oystercatchers can be seen on an incoming tide along the rocky shore.

BOTANIC GARDENS AT SAMARÈS MANOR

Before returning to St Helier, it is well worth making a mile (1.6km) detour north to **Samarès Manor** ⑧ (www.samaresmanor.com;

The tranquil water garden has a soothing effect on the visitor.

soon see signs to the manor, off to the right. The name "Samarès" derives from the Old Norman French *Salse Marais*, or saltwater marsh, dating from ancient times when the owners profited from the saltpans on the low-lying land to the south.

Today they make their money from tourism, attracting large numbers of visitors to the alluring gardens that surround the manor house.

The original grounds were designed by Sir James Knott, Tyneside ship owner and philanthropist, who spent the last 10 years of his life in Jersey. His enthusiasm for Eastern-style planting is reflected in the exotic Japanese-style rock and water gardens. But Samarès has seen a major program of restoration and diversification over the years, and now there are over 14 acres (6 hectares) of gardens to explore, as well as a plant trail and guided tours of the Jersey Rural Life and Carriage Museum.

A highlight is the **Herb Garden**, uniquely designed and filled with fragrant, medicinal and culinary plants. The Herb Café is a lovely spot to take a break, sited amid the culinary herbs

Apr–mid-Oct daily 9.30am–5pm, guided tours of the Manor, Mon-Sat, 11.30am and 2pm, and of the Rural Life and Carriage Museum daily 10.30am and 3.30pm), highlight of the parish of St Clement. From Green Island take the narrow Rue de Samarès going north, and turn left when you reach the main A5. You'll

A Marine Wilderness

The Jersey Ramsar Site, stretching from St Helier Harbour to Gorey Pier, is a marine wilderness, characterised by weather-worn reefs, mud, sand and shingle shores, and exposed twice daily by one of the largest tidal ranges in the world.

The Gulf Stream-warmed waters are home to a rich and valuable ecology. Some 107 species of fish, 57 of crustacea, 113 of mollusc and 230 of seaweed have been recorded – far more than the criteria set by Ramsar.

The gulf stream provides a perfect nutrient-rich breeding ground for oysters.

Victor Hugo gathers inspiration at Le Dicq.

which are used to flavour the dishes. Parts of the manor house, where the owners live, can be visited on guided tours (Mon–Sat).

LE DICQ AND VICTOR HUGO

Turn right out of Samarès on to the A5 and you will soon be back on the A4 and the outskirts of St Helier. Just beyond where the two roads merge, on the seaward side, Le Dicq slipway has a plaque to **Victor Hugo**, who lived nearby.

In 1851, when Louis Napoleon staged a coup in France, the French writer and staunch Republican feared for his life and fled from France. He

A plaque in honour of Victor Hugo, at La Pomme d'Or Hotel, St Helier.

chose Jersey, which had a history of granting asylum to refugees – the Prince of Wales (later Charles II), Huguenots and Royalist revolutionaries among them.

Hugo stayed at La Pomme d'Or Hotel in St Helier until he was able to find a house by the sea. He lived with his wife and children at 3 Marina Terrace, Greve d'Azette, while his mistress, Juliette Drouais, was conveniently lodged just down the road at Le Havre des Pas.

Hugo's house, which was knocked down in the 1970s, was fairly spartan, but he was close to Le Dicq where he drew inspiration from the sea. He gathered here with other exiles by a large rock, accessible at low tide, known as Le Rocher des Proscrits. In 1855 the exiles' Jersey newspaper, *L'Homme*, published a letter discrediting Queen Victoria for making a state visit to Louis Napoleon – by this time Napoleon III. Jersey was (and still is) supportive of the monarchy and the editor and owner of the newspaper were expelled from the island without trial.

Hugo signed a declaration against the expulsion and as a result was forced to set sail for Guernsey, where he lived for the next 15 years.

Eating Out

St Saviour

Le Dicq

Thai Dicq Shack

Dicq Slipway, Dicq Road, St Saviour; tel: 01534-730 273; summer daily noon–9pm, winter 5–9pm.

Dig your toes in the sand and tuck into fresh and fabulous Thai food. Bring your own drinks. Takeaway available most of the year. £

Longueville Manor

Longueville Road; tel: 01534-725 501; www.longuevillemanor.com; lunch and dinner daily.

Exclusive country hotel offering a haven of indulgence. Come for gourmet cuisine, with local seasonal produce from the kitchen garden, and exceptional service and hospitality. £££

St Catherine's Bay

Breakwater Café

La Route de St Catherine; tel: 01534-851 141; daily 8am–5pm.

Popular spot after a bracing walk along the pier to sit and watch the boats go by. Homely and unpretentious with classic café menu, all-day breakfasts and popular ice-cream parlour. £

Grouville

Bass and Lobster Foodhouse

Gorey Coast Road, St Martin; tel: 01534-859 590; www.bassandlobster. com; Tue–Sat lunch and dinner.

Roger White, one of Jersey's best-known chefs, is well-known for championing Jersey produce, whether it's hand-dived scallops, chancre crab or line-caught sea bass. Despite the name there are always meat dishes available, many of which are locally sourced. £££

Crab Shack

La Route de la Côte, Gorey (opposite the castle); tel: 01534-850 830; www.jerseycrabshack.com; Apr–Sept lunch and dinner daily, Oct–Mar Tue–Sat lunch and dinner, Sun lunch only.

The old Castle Green pub is now the sister of the St Brelade Crab Shack (see page 45). It's well worth the trek up for excellent seafood and fine views of the bay. ££

Feast

Gorey Pier; tel: 01534-611 118; www. feast.je; Wed–Mon lunch and dinner.

An island favourite, specialising in simple freshly cooked cuisine, from the signature sticky ribs to imaginative salads and delicious seafood. Excellent options for vegetarians. ££

Suma's

Gorey Hill; tel: 01534-853 291; www. sumasrestaurant.com; Mon–Sat lunch and dinner, Sat–Sun breakfast 9.30–11am.

Fresh, innovative cuisine in a stylish little restaurant overlooking Gorey harbour and castle – reserve a table alfresco. British dishes with a twist of Mediterranean flair and legendary weekend brunch. Book in advance, especially if you want a terrace table with outstanding views of Grouville Bay and Gorey Castle. ££–£££

Green Island

Green Island Restaurant and Beach Hut

Green Island; tel: 01534-857 787; www.greenisland.je; Restaurant: Tue–Sun noon–2.30pm, 6.30–9.30pm, Beach Hut Tue–Sun 9am–5pm.

Soak up the sea views and enjoy sensational seafood. Vegetarians and meat eaters are also catered for. Friendly, fun atmosphere. ££–£££

Flamingos add a splash of colour to the grounds of Les Augrès Manor.

Tour 7

Durrell's Wildlife

"You can't build a tortoise. You can't build a bird. That's what we've got to remember – if we destroy it, we can't recreate it." Gerald Durrell (1925–95)

From the age of six, when he lived in central India, Gerald Durrell kept a collection of animals and dreamt of having his own zoo. His first collection included "everything from minnows to woodlice"; then, when his family moved to Corfu during the 1930s, his menagerie extended to "everything from eagle owls to scorpions". His animal adventures on the Greek island – along with the antics of his family – are humorously described in his best-selling book *My Family and Other Animals* (1956). The hit TV series The Durrells (2016-18) was based on Durrell's three autobiographical books about his years living on the Greek island of Corfu.

At 21 Durrell inherited £3,000 and used it to fund an animal-collecting expedition to the British Cameroons. In 1957, after several other major expeditions to far-flung parts

This way for flamingos and gorillas, that way for bats and lemurs.

Les Augrès Manor, once Durrell's home, is now the headquarters of the Durrell Wildlife Conservation Trust.

of the world to collect animals on behalf of zoos, the pioneering naturalist and author founded what was then known as the Jersey Wildlife Preservation Trust. The name was later changed to the Durrell Wildlife Conservation Trust, then to the Durrell Wildlife Park – or simply Durrell - and now it is called Jersey Zoo. For many years this has been the island's prime visitor attraction. This is no ordinary zoo with the usual elephants and giraffes. It is entirely devoted to the preservation of animal life and has become internationally renowned as a sanctuary and breeding centre for some of the world's most endangered species.

DURRELL'S LEGACY

For over 60 years the Trust has been working on saving species from extinction, building up colonies and reintroducing them to their original homes. As the symbol of the Trust Durrell chose the dodo, demonstrating his commitment to saving rare species from the fate of the flightless bird from Mauritius.

Durrell Souvenirs

The Durrell shop has an excellent range of animal-related products, including Gerald Durrell's books (he wrote no less than 37) including *My Family and Other Animals* (his amusing animal adventures on Corfu), zoo videos, limited edition ceramics, gorilla posters, soft toy orang-utans, Livingstone fruit bats and lemurs, jigsaws and souvenirs with the Durrell (dodo) symbol.

Feeding time is a popular time, not just for the animals, but the visitors too.

In the early days Durrell's efforts at captive breeding were dismissed by many eminent zoologists. He was one of the first to draw attention to what was happening in the environment, and 50 years on virtually every reputable zoo follows at least some of the principles that he put into practice here in Jersey.

Visitor Information

Getting There: Jersey Zoo, Les Augrès Manor, La Profonde Rue, Trinity (4 miles/6km north of St Helier), accessed on the B31; tel: 01534-860 000; www.durrell.org. Bus routes: 3, 4, 13 and 23.
Admission: Open daily 9.30am–6pm (5pm in winter). Guided tours (English, French or German) must be pre-booked four working days in advance. Tours are given by volunteers, and a discretionary donation is suggested towards upkeep of the zoo. Trained guides are also located around the site and are happy to answer any questions you might have.

THE PERFECT SETTING

Since the zoo opened in 1959 over 13,000 animals have been born here, and several species have been saved from extinction and reintroduced into their original habitats. Gerald Durrell died in 1995, and at his memorial service David Attenborough spoke of the zoo's priorities: "the animals first, the staff second and the public as privileged paying guests". Durrell's zoologist wife, Lee, is executor of the Durrell estate and continues the work of the Trust.

Durrell's famous memoirs.

White-handed gibbons move around by swinging their body along using alternate handholds.

A Sumatran orang-utan collects his take-away lunch.

Among other projects are the **Floreana mockingbird** from the Galápagos and the **Montserrat mountain chicken**, a large frog that is in danger of extinction from a fungal disease. Closer to home, Durrell works with local wildlife groups to help save the declining population of Jersey's green lizard and the symbolic Jersey *crapaud* or common toad.

A moated enclosure near the entrance is home to a family of ring-tailed coatis and a much-loved and long-established pair of **Andean bears**, Wolfgang and Barbara. The only bears in South America, the species is being pushed to extinction by the destruction of their natural habitats and the huge demand for bear blood, bile and organs used in traditional medicine and delicacies such as bear paw soup.

GENTLE JAMBO

Favourite inmates of the zoo are the **Sumatran orang-utans**, who

ly concentrating on restoring the ecosystems of the small islands of Mauritius that were once rich habitats of wildlife. Other species which have been brought back from the brink are the **golden lion tamarins** which have been released in a private reserve in Brazil, the **thick-billed parrots**, considered extinct in Arizona, which are now flying free in their native pinewoods, the **St Lucia whiptail lizard**, the **Mallorcan midwife toad** and the **Assam pygmy hog**, the smallest pig in the world.

In 1989 a pair of **St Lucia Amazon parrots**, the national bird, flew courtesy of British Airways back to the Caribbean, accompanied by the Prime Minister of St Lucia who travelled to Jersey especially to escort them home.

Adopt an Animal

It was Durrell's dream to close down the Trust because it would no longer be necessary, as there weren't any endangered species. But he knew it wouldn't happen. "The world is being destroyed at the speed of an Exocet missile, and we are riding a bicycle," he said of his work. "I feel despair 24 hours a day." The Trust was – and still is – plagued by financial problems and as a charity depends on public help. You can give support by adopting an animal, becoming a member, donating to Durrell or buying a souvenir (further information at www.durrell.org).

Animal Experiences

At Jersey Zoo you can do more than just see the animals. There are options to roll up your sleeves and be a keeper for the day, help to feed the animals, muck in and make them feel at home. Or choose from 'Animal Experiences', meeting the meerkats, bears, apes or reptiles. See www.durrell.org for more information and costs.

provide endless entertainment in their splendid habitat of islands and waterways; the **Livingstone fruit bats**, with a wingspan of 6ft (almost 2 metres); and – most famous of all – the **western lowland gorillas**.

Beside the compound a statue commemorates Jambo, the mighty silver-back gorilla who shot to international stardom in 1986 when he stood over a five-year-old boy who fell into the enclosure, protecting him from the rest of the gorillas. The "gentle giant", who fathered 13 offspring and died in 1992, was the

Bronze statue of Jambo, the "gentle giant".

first male gorilla to be reared in captivity.

For a unique experience animal lovers can camp out in luxury at the Durrell Wildlife Camp (see page 125), with unlimited access to the park.

Oriental short-clawed otters live in the re-developed valley.

Cycle routes in Jersey

Sea kayaking in Jersey's clear waters.

Travel Tips

Active Pursuits

From surfing and skydiving to fishing and golf, Jersey has a host of activities to keep you occupied.

Sports enthusiasts are spoilt for choice on Jersey, whether it's on the water or ashore. In an effort to rejuvenate its image, the island has introduced a range of adventure sports in recent years. Along with the usual, long-established activities such as surfing and sailing, you can try out sports such as skydiving, blokarting, kiteboarding, abseiling and stand-up paddle-boarding. The Visit Jersey website (www.jersey.com) is packed with information on all the activities on the island and the companies which operate them.

WALKING

Jersey has a walk for every day of the year, from dramatic rugged cliffs to the leafy lanes of the interior. The island may be small, but it offers some surprisingly dramatic and varied scenery, particularly along the northern coastline. Here the footpath follows the coast for most of the way, dipping down to fishing villages where you can take a break at beachside cafés.

Jersey Tourism publishes a free pamphlet with ideas for walks, from north coast walking routes to reservoir walks and 'Ice Age' trails, with a map provided. Specialist guided walks are numerous, with themes ranging from Victorian Jersey and World War II to the Oyster Trail and hidden gardens. One of the most fascinating is the "moonwalk", taking you across the lunar-like seascape at the south-eastern tip of the island. This gigantic rock pool disappears below the sea twice a day. Information on guided walks can be found at www.jersey.com.

For self-guided walks, forget the car and get around the island with

The Railway Walk

The now defunct Western Railway track, linking St Helier with St Aubin and later extended to La Corbière, has been turned into a foot and cycle path. This makes an enjoyable, unchallenging walk (or cycle ride) ending up at La Corbière, where you can walk out to the lighthouse providing the tide is not too high. If you do not want to make the return journey on foot, buses will take you back to St Aubin or St Helier.

Some of the finest walks are to be found in Jersey, both along the coast and inland.

the help of the excellent bus service. Timetables are available from the tourist office or bus station in St Helier, or at www.libertybus.je. The best map is the Ordnance Survey-style Jersey Official Leisure Map. When exploring the coast, visitors should watch out for extreme tidal movement, one of the largest recorded in the world.

Inland walks

The rural interior offers walks through woodlands, valleys and reservoirs. The path alongside Waterworks Valley, running north from Millbrook, follows the winding road past reservoirs and through wooded slopes. To the west, the Jersey War Tunnels (www.jersey wartunnels.com) is a good starting point for walks through attractive woodland along St Peter's Valley. In the northeast of the island, there are delightful walks in the thickly wooded valley of Rozel Woods, between St Catherine's Bay and St Martin's Village. The path circling the Y-shaped Val de la Mare reservoir is an easy 3-mile (5km) walk, providing fine views of the distant St Ouen's Bay from near the dam. Queen's Valley Reservoir, west of

Gorey, provides another pleasant, undemanding walk which takes you around the trout-filled waters.

In the third week of June keen hikers flock to Jersey for the Itex 48-mile (77km) walk around the island. Expect to complete the course in anything between 12–21 hours. Funds go to Jersey charities.

CYCLING

No distance on Jersey is too far to cycle, and the network of quiet country lanes and coastal roads makes for pleasant, if at times stren-

Walking in Rozel Woods.

uous, cycling. A 96-mile (155km) network has been established all over the island, and the clear signs along the way enable you to explore the winding lanes without constantly referring to maps. The routes take in the Green Lanes, where pedestrians, cyclists and horse-riders have priority over cars, and motorists must slow down to a sedate 15mph (24kmh). If a rural lane suddenly ceases to be a Green Lane, the probability is you have cycled across a parish boundary; two parishes (Trinity and St Saviour) are still resisting the Green Lane scheme.

Visitors who want to plan their own cycling itineraries should consult the Visit Jersey website (www. jersey.com) for detailed cycling routes. The Island Tourist Map includes cycle routes marking the coastal circuit, inland links and connections to various popular attractions. For private guided cycle tours contact Arthur Lamy, an experienced cycle tourist guide, at www. arthurthebluebadgeguide.com.

For cycle hire, see Practical Information (see page 118).

SURFING

St Ouen's Bay, with its huge rollers and spacious sands, is a paradise for surfers. The first surf club to open here was the Jersey Surfboard Club (www.jerseysurfboardclub.com) – established in 1959 and one of the first in Europe. This and other clubs hire out surf equipment and offer tuition. You can also learn to kitesurf, propelling yourself at high speeds across the sea on a surfboard with a large controllable kite.

Bodyboarding is hugely popular along the bay, from the old guard who still use wooden boards to youngsters in wetsuits with the latest gear. Equipment can be hired at any of the surf schools. The seas are rough, with rip tides and strong currents. Inexperienced surfers should always keep to the areas between flags, which are patrolled by lifeguards. Red flags indicate the conditions are dangerous.

Experienced windsurfers enjoy skimming along the sea at St Ouen's, but the more sheltered bays of St Brelade's Bay, St Aubin's or Grouville are a lot more suitable for learners. The

Kitesurfing at St Ouen's Bay.

Casting off on the rocks at St Catherine's Bay.

Free Guided Walks

The National Trust (www. nationaltrust.je) offers free guided walks with emphasis on Jersey's heritage and environment. Every year Visit Jersey hosts the spring and autumn walking festivals (second week of May and third week of September respectively), with free walks for all abilities and ages. Some of the walks celebrate food which is produced, grown or made in Jersey, for example oyster fishing, classic cattle, Jersey Royals, wine tasting or cheese production.

water sports centres on these bays also offer paddle -boarding, waterskiing, wakeboarding, banana rides, rowing boats and canoes.

SAILING

Marinas and harbours have excellent facilities for sailors but beginners should beware of sunken reefs, big tides and strong currents. Experienced sailors can charter boats or join local regattas. For yacht charter, private skippered charter trips, catamaran island tours or learning to sail contact Go Sail (www.go-sail.je).

SEA KAYAKING/ COASTEERING

Jersey's clear waters, remote coves and rich marine life make for excellent kayaking and coasteering (scrambling around the rocks, cliff jumping and swimming through caves). The kayak specialists are Jersey Kayak Adventures (www.jerseykayakadventures. co.uk) who operate from beaches all over the island. Pure Adventure (www.purejersey.com) on St Brelade's Bay organize coasteering, sea kayaking, blokarting, wakeboarding and other adventure sports.

FISHING

Sea bass, wrasse, grey mullet, bream, pollack and mackerel and occasionally conger eel are caught offshore. For deep-sea fishing trips, by day or night, contact David Nuth, tel: 01534-858 046 or 07797-728 316 (www.tarka seatrips.com). The piers on the north coast are popular for rod fishing.

For young children there are numerous rock pools where you can catch crabs, shrimps and devil fish. Every beach shop sells cheap nets

Cider barrels at Hamptonne Country Life Museum.

Leisure and Fitness

Keep in trim at Fitness First at the Waterfront Centre in St Helier, equipped with gym, cardio theatre, spinning room, sauna, steam room and beauty room. The next door Aqua Splash has a 25-metre, six-lane swimming pool, and outdoor pool with flumes, slides and diving area.

Aqua Splash has indoor and outdoor pools.

and buckets. At St Aubin's Bay during spring tides you can sprinkle salt on the keyhole-shaped burrow of razor fish and watch them pop up out of their holes.

DIVING

The sea in Jersey is clean, visibility is good and marine life plentiful. Most of the diving takes place at Bouley Bay on the north coast, where the waters are particularly clear and conditions normally calm. The Bouley Bay Diving School (www.scubadivingjersey.com) is a PADI 5-star diving centre which welcomes divers of all standards, including beginners. More experienced divers can visit the wrecks of ships sunk in World War II and other vessels which have been scuttled to provide shelter for marine life.

BEACHES AND SWIMMING

The water temperatures are on the cool side (averaging around 17°C/63°F in summer), which does have the advantage that the seas are crowd-free. The beaches are clean, with clear waters, but beware of currents and tides. The main beach-

A hole-in-one at the Royal Jersey Golf Club.

Playing soldiers on the assault course at Valley Adventure Centre.

es are surveyed by lifeguards during the season. The best beaches for youngsters are St Brelade's, St Aubin and Grouville, where the sand shelves gently and the waters are normally calm. Beauport, west of St Brelade's, accessed down a steep path, is one of the least crowded bays.

GOLF

The island has six golf courses. Top of the list is the Royal Jersey Golf Club (www.royaljersey.com) beside Royal Grouville Bay. The club was founded in 1878 and was the training ground of Grouville-born Harry Vardon, six times winner of the British Open. You need proof of handicap to play here, as you do for La Moye Golf Club at St Brelade (www.lamoyegolfclub.co.uk), which has some stunning views of St Ouen's Bay. Non-club members can play at the 18-hole Les Mielles Golf and Country Club (www.lesmielles.com), the 9-hole courses at Wheatlands, St Peter (www.wheatlandsjersey.com) or Les Ormes, St Brelade (www.lesormesjersey.co.uk).

Blokarting at St Ouen's Bay.

Valley Adventure Centre

This exhilarating activity centre (www.valleyadventure.je) is set in a natural green valley, and provides a host of adventurous pursuits for children and adults. You can try out aerial trekking, abseiling, freefall jumping, zip wire, military-style assault course, laser combat – to name just a few.

Themed Holidays

Themes on Jersey range from German Occupation War trails to yoga retreats by the beach.

HERITAGE HOLIDAYS

Leger Holidays (tel: 01709-787 463; www.leger.co.uk) organise 5- or 8-day residential Occupation and Liberation tours, with the opportunity to talk to a number of islanders who lived through the Occupation.

Jersey Heritage Holidays (tel: 01534-862 099; www.jerseyheritage-holidays.com) offer residential holidays of specialist interest (German Occupation and Liberation, self-guided walking tours, history, and flora and fauna). The company organises hotel accommodation but clients make their own travel arrangements.

WALKING TOURS

With **Macs Adventure** (www.macs adventure.com) you can go round the entire island on foot in a week (March to October only). Bed and breakfast accommodation and door-to-door luggage transfer are included.

SPA AND GASTRONOMY

The Club Hotel & Spa (tel: 01534-876 500; www.theclubjersey. com), St Helier's luxury boutique hotel, offers spa packages combining a morning at the Club Spa's thermal suite, a swim in the indoor saltwater poor (or private outdoor pool) and a three-course lunch at the hotel's gourmet Bohemia restaurant.

SPORTS

Young would-be surfers can join non-residential summer camps with **Jersey Quicksilver Surf School** (tel: 01534-484 005; www.jerseysurf school.co.uk). Five-day courses for 8- to 16-year-olds, either full days or 2 hours a day. The Valley Adventure Centre (www.valleyadventure.je) runs all-year activity clubs for 7-14 year-olds which include aerial trekking, zip wire assault course, and spring and summer water sports. Full week: £285, single day: £58.

BUSH CAMPS

Discover wild edible and medicinal plants, cook on a beach fire, learn natural navigating skills, make cordage using plants and trees and construct your own shelter. Activities include rock climbing, coasteering, abseiling, boogie-boarding and cycle tours. The overnight location is off the beaten track in a lovely part of the island. Overnight or 6-day survival courses. For more information contact Kazz at **Wild Adventures** (07797-886 242; www.wildadventuresjersey.com)

CONSERVATION

Put something back into the environment with practical conservation work by volunteering for the National Trust's scheme (tel: 01534-483 193; www.nationaltrust.je).

ARTS

Jersey Arts Centre (www.artscen tre.je) runs occasional non-residential art courses and workshops for both children and adults.

Outdoor pool at The Club Hotel & Spa

Practical Information

GETTING THERE

Year-round air and sea packages, short breaks, flights and accommodation can all be arranged through specialist tour operators such as Jersey Travel (tel: 03300-299 497; www.jerseytravel.com) and Channel Islands Direct (tel: 0800-640 9058; www.channelislandsdirect. co.uk).

Condor Ferries can arrange sea packages and short breaks (tel: 01621-734 111; www.condor breaks.com). If you have booked accommodation independently, your hotel can normally arrange transport for you, as well as car rental if required. Visit Jersey (www. jersey.com) has detailed information of air and sea travel, plus a list of specialist tour operators.

By air

During the summer direct flights to Jersey operate from around 40 UK airports. From London airports alone there are up to 12 flights a day. Off season the number of flights is reduced, especially from regional airports. The main airlines are Flybe (www.flybe.com), which operate flights from London Gatwick and around 20 other UK airports, easyJet (www.easyjet.com), which flies from Gatwick, Luton, Southend, Liverpool, Newcastle, Belfast. Edinburgh and Glasgow, and British Airways (www.ba.com), which operate regular flights from Gatwick. There are no airlines operating direct services from London Heathrow.

Many tour operators also offer seasonal charter flights from UK regional airports. For further information click on "Getting Here" on the Visit Jersey website (www.jersey.

com). The best prices are normally secured by booking well in advance on the internet and avoiding weekends and the busiest times of year. Both Aurigny (www.aurigny. com) and Blue Islands (www.blueislands.com) provide a Channel Island hopping service between Jersey and Guernsey; Aurigny also includes Alderney.

Jersey airport (www.jerseyairport.com) is 5 miles (8km) west of St Helier in St Peter. Car hire and taxis are available, and a bus (No. 15) leaves every 20 minutes (30 minutes in winter) for St Helier.

By sea

The only ferry line from the UK to Jersey is Condor Ferries (tel: 01621-734 111; www.condorferries.co.uk), which operates a high-speed ferry service from Poole. The crossing normally goes via Guernsey and takes 4 hours and 30 minutes. It is not uncommon for boats to be cancelled or delayed because of the

The Commodore Clipper.

weather conditions, particularly off season. The state-of-the-art trimaran, Condor *Liberation* accommodates 850 passengers and 235 cars, and has on board a cafeteria, bars, soft play area for children and a duty-free shop with some excellent deals, especially on alcohol. Club-class seating and steward service is available for an extra charge.

Condor Ferries also operates a slower service from Portsmouth on the conventional Commodore car/passenger ferry. The crossing takes 8–11 hours, depending on whether the ferry stops at Guernsey. The return crossing is overnight with the option of 1-, 2-, 3- or 4-berth cabins and en suite facilities.

Fast ferry services from Jersey to Guernsey and St Malo in France are also operated by Condor Ferries.

Visitors bringing their own car must have the vehicle registration document and a valid driving licence or International Driving Permit (photocopies not accepted). Bikes can be taken across free of charge.

GETTING AROUND

Buses

Jersey has an efficient, easy-to-use network of buses, operated by Liberty Bus (tel: 01534-828 555; www.libertybus.je). All buses radiate from Liberation Station, St Helier. Bus timetables, with a map of the routes and a Liberation Station layout plan, are available from either the bus station, or the nearby tourist office. The website has a journey planner and gives live times. To find out from your mobile when the next bus is due to arrive text the four-digit number at the bus stop to 6656. Tickets can be bought on board. A Hop-on Hop-off ticket allows unlimited travel for 1, 2, 3 or 7 days and is available from Liberty Station.

Half-day, evening and whole-day island coach tours are available with a pick-up service from many hotels. Visit Tantivy Blue Coach Tours (www.tantivybluecoach.com) or Waverley Coaches (www.waverleycoaches.co.uk).

The choice is yours.

The amphibious Castle Ferry at Elizabeth Castle, St Helier.

Car hire

To hire a car you need to be at least 20 and hold a valid driving licence with no endorsements for dangerous or drunken driving in the last five years. Most companies impose an upper age limit. Rental prices in Jersey are similar to those in the UK and petrol prices slightly cheaper. Car hire companies are abundant and competitive.

Hire firms include: Avis (freephone: 0800-735 1110; www.avisjersey. co.uk), Europcar (freephone: 0800-735 0735; www.europcarjersey.com), Hertz, Jersey Airport (tel: 01534-636 666; www.hertz.co.uk) and the local company Zebra Hire (9 Esplanade, St Helier; tel: 01534-736 556; www. zebrahire.com). Free-phone numbers are from UK only.

Driving

The island's maximum speed limit is 40mph (64kmh), reduced to 30mph or 20mph (48 or 32kmh) in some town areas and to 15mph (24kmh) on Green Lanes, where priority is given to pedestrians and cyclists. Rules of the road are the same as those of the UK: driving is on the left, seat belts are compulsory, and

it is an offence to hold a mobile phone whilst driving. Fixed alcohol limits and roadside breath testing are similar to the UK. Penalties are severe, with up to £2,000 fine or 6 months' imprisonment for the first offence plus unlimited disqualification of your driving licence.

Cycling is an environmentally friendly way of exploring the island.

Green Flag

Jersey was the first holiday destination in the world to be awarded Green Globe Status in recognition of schemes such as the Green Lane network, coastal footpaths and cycle tracks. On the other hand Jersey has one of the highest ratios of cars to people in the world, and this, coupled with the high population density, puts pressure on the environment and infrastructure. The best bet for going green is to travel to Jersey by ferry, cycle around the island or use the network of buses.

Cycle-route signs.

Parking requires the use of either a yellow disco or Paycard, available from Visit Jersey, Condor Ferries, hire-car companies, post offices, shops or anywhere displaying the Paycard logo (a blue P inside a red C). The cards are available as individual units or in books of ten. PayByPhone, available in all paying public car parks, is a cashless service which allows you to pay for parking using your mobile phone.

Cycling

See Active Pursuits, page 109. Bikes can be hired from Zebra Hire (9 The Esplanade St Helier; tel: 01534-736 556; www.zebra hire.com) or from Jersey Bike Hire, (www.jerseybikehire.co.uk). If you are travelling with Condor Ferries, bikes can be brought over from the UK free of charge.

Inter-island ferries and France

Condor (see also "By Sea") operate a high-speed car ferry service between St Malo and Jersey (2hrs 20 minutes). From April to September Manche-îles-express (tel: 01534-

880 756; www.manche-iles-ex press.com) operate services from St Helier to Sark and to Carteret, Granville and Diélette in Normandy, and from Gorey to Carteret and Diélette Passports are required for France.

There is a good supply of cycle shops and hire facilities in Jersey.

Condor Ferries operate day trips to Guernsey, with ferry connections on to Sark and Herm.

Taxis

Taxis on Jersey are expensive. Ranks are located at the airport, harbour and St Helier. Otherwise call Citicabs: 01534-499 999; Domino Cabs: 01534-747 047; or Liberty Cabs: 01534-767 700.

FACTS FOR THE VISITOR

Disabled travellers

For detailed information covering accommodation, transport, parking, attractions and equipment for hire for the disabled, visit www.jersey com/accessible-jersey. On-street parking and public car parks have designated areas for UK and European Blue Badge holders. Public conveniences for the disabled, fitted with radar locks, can be found in all the main centres and at most beaches. Keys can be collected at the Jersey Visitor Centre in St Helier, Shopmobility in Sand Street car park or the Town Hall. A refundable £5 deposit is required. See also Beachability (www.beachability.org, tel: 07797-935 088) who may be able to provide a special wheelchair for beach access. Apart from the Sand Street car park a shopmobility scheme operates at Durrell Wildlife Conservation Trust and Jersey War Tunnels (see www.shopmobility. org.je). Prior booking is advisable.

Emergencies

Dial 999 for police, fire, ambulance or coastal rescue services. The General Hospital at The Parade, St Helier (tel: 01534-442 000) has a 24-hour emergency unit. The UK has a reciprocal arrangement entitling UK visitors to free health care in Jersey. The agreement does not cover certain types of follow-on treatment or travel costs, however.

Myriad sights to see on the island.

The pound is the official unit of currency in Jersey.

Money

The pound sterling is the currency of the island. Jersey has its own currency, in the same denominations as UK notes and coins, apart from the fact it still has £1 notes. Jersey money can be used on any of the other Channel Islands but is sometimes refused by shops in the UK. Notes can be changed at the airport bank or any bank in the UK. Some shops also accept euros. All major debit and credit cards are widely accepted. ATMs are readily available in St Helier, St Saviour, St Peter, Red Houses, the airport and harbour.

Opening times

Bank opening times are generally the same as those in the UK. Most of the museums and tourist attractions are open Apr–Oct, some Mar–Nov, daily 9am or 10am–5pm. The main post office, on Broad Street, St Helier, is open Mon–Fri 8.30am–5pm (opens 9am on Tue), Sat 8.30am–1pm. Normal shopping hours are Monday to Saturday 9am–5.30pm, though a number of shops, particularly in St Helier, are also open in the evenings and Liberty Wharf in St Helier is open seven days a week. Markets and some shops are closed on Thursday afternoons.

Telephones

The code of Jersey is 01534 from the British Isles, +44 1534 from any other country. STD codes for the UK from Jersey are the same as those used in the UK. But if you are using a mobile phone beware that Jersey does not work on the UK system. The networks require a roaming facility, and there are charges for making and receiving texts and calls. Some "Pay as You Go" phones do not operate in Jersey, so check with your provider before you go. The three Jersey networks are JT Global – which has the best coverage – Airtel-Vodafone and

Telephone boxes are painted bright yellow and easily identifiable.

Let's have another round of the local smooth bitter.

Sure. The network extends to the other Channel Islands. Visitors with mobiles will either be linked automatically to a network or can select the network manually.

Tourist information

Visit Jersey (Liberation Place, St Helier; tel: 01534-859 000; www.jersey.com) has a wealth of information on the island and can also arrange accommodation.

Entertainment

The Jersey Opera House, Gloucester Street, St Helier (www.jerseyoperahouse.co.uk) stages drama, dance, ballet, concerts, musicals, very occasional opera and children's shows. A registered charity and non-profit organisation, the Jersey Arts Centre (Phillips Street, St Helier; www.artscentre.je) offers a wide range of contemporary and classic performing and visual arts.

Nightlife is mainly confined to St Helier and consists of pubs and discos primarily aimed at young residents. The *Jersey Post* is the best place to find out about performances by live bands, jazz concerts, DJs, etc. Focal areas are The Weighbridge and Liberty Wharf. The Drift Bar in the Royal Yacht Hotel has a cool ambience, and live music and DJs; Mimosa in Liberty Wharf has a Champagne and cocktail bar and terrace overlooking the marina.

Travel documents and customs allowances

No passport is required for visitors travelling from the British Isles and the Republic of Ireland, but airlines require passengers to have photographic ID. A passport is required if you take a day trip to France. Jersey is not part of the EU, so you can still buy duty-free goods when travelling to and from the island. Maximum allowances are: 200 cigarettes or 250grams of other tobacco products; 1 litre of spirits or 4 litres of sparkling or fortified wines and 4 litres of still wines; 16 litres of beer; £390 worth of perfumes, gifts, souvenirs, electrical products and similar items.

Accommodation

From quirky B&Bs and yurts to to country manors and luxury spa hotels, Jersey caters for all tastes.

To rejuvenate Jersey's image several of the top hotels have undergone multi-million-pound revamps, and a quarter of the hotel guest rooms are now within the 4- and 5-star range. This is all good news if your pockets are well-lined; finding cheap accommodation in Jersey is not so easy.

The self-catering scene in Jersey has been looking up in recent years with more seaside accommodation to rent and, for the adventurous, the opportunity to stay in historic monuments and follies which have been restored by Jersey Heritage (www.jerseyheritage.org). These range from "stone hut" accommodation in 19th-century seafront fortresses or towers to a stylish 1930s boat-shaped folly on the beach and a panoramic German Occupation observation tower.

To find the best deals book online, either through Visit Jersey or specialist operators (see page 126), or choose your hotel and book direct through them. It's worth comparing costs – sometimes a package through the hotel can work out to be the cheapest option. Typical special offers are three nights for the price of two or free car hire for stays of at least three nights. Off-season room rates can fall dramatically, and there are some great deals at some of the hotels that remain open in winter.

For rooms in July and August book well ahead. Supplements are nearly always charged for sea-view rooms. Check the cost – it's often worth a little extra per night for the fabulous view you could wake up to.

WHERE TO STAY

St Helier isn't the most attractive centre on Jersey, and budget accommodation is limited; but it does have the best sightseeing and shopping, and buses from here will take you all over the island.

Many holidaymakers prefer to stay in smaller centres such as the picturesque ports of St Aubin or Gorey, or on the beautiful beach of St Brelade's. All three have an excellent choice of restaurants and good bus links.

HOTELS

The price bands below are a guideline for the cost of a standard en suite double room and breakfast for two people in high season (July–Aug).
£££ = over £220
££ = £110 -£220
£ = under £110

You'll be spoilt for choice by the many fine dining opportunities on offer.

Luxurious bedroom at The Club Hotel & Spa.

St Helier
Club Hotel and Spa
Green Street; tel: 01534-876 500; www.theclubjersey.com.
Luxury boutique hotel, with 38 rooms and eight suites. Chic decor, a swish spa and outdoor swimming pool, and the highest rated restaurant on the island. £££

La Bonne Vie
Roseville Street; tel: 01534-735 955.
Charming Victorian guesthouse close to Havre des Pas beach and swimming pool. Homely atmosphere with flowers everywhere and individually furnished guest rooms, some featuring antique brass and French four-poster beds. £

Grand Jersey Hotel & Spa
The Esplanade, tel: 01534-720 371; www.handpickedhotels.co.uk/Grand-Jersey
Swish and glamorous 5-star hotel where you can sip vintage bubbles in the Champagne Lounge, dine in the seductive Tassili restaurant and wind down or work out in the stylish Elemis spa and pool. ££

Monterey Hotel
St Saviour's Road; tel: 01534-873 006; www.morvanhotels.com.
Just a 10-minute walk from the centre of town, the Monterey offers comfortable modern accommodation and excellent leisure facilities. Main features include indoor and outdoor pools, spa pool, steam room and mini-gym. ££

Royal Yacht
Weighbridge; tel: 01534-720 511; www.theroyalyacht.com.
One of Jersey's oldest hotels; built in the 1930s, now a stylish modern hotel. Café Zephyr is a favourite of fashionistas, Sirocco offers fine dining, the P.O.S.H. Bar is the place for bubbles, the Drift for live music and cool ambience. Luxury spa, gym and indoor pool. £££

St Aubin's Bay and St Aubin
Harbour View
St Aubin's Harbour; tel: 01534-741 585; www.harbourviewjersey.com.
Charming, relaxed guesthouse across the road from the harbour.

Watch the sunset at the Atlantic Hotel in St Brelade's.

Snacks are served on the garden terrace, and there are plenty of options for dining out nearby. ££

Millbrook House

Rue de Trachy, Millbrook; tel: 01534-733 036; www.millbrookhousehotel.com.

This is a peaceful retreat, surrounded by 10 acres (4 hectares) of park and gardens, halfway between St Helier and St Aubin. Traditional decor, discreet service and very reasonable prices. £

The Panorama

La Rue du Crocquet, St Aubin; tel: 01534-742 429; www.panoramajersey.com.

Award-winning B&B with fine bay views from picture windows, luxury beds and excellent breakfasts. Non-smoking and adults-only. Plenty of restaurants close by. ££

St Brelade's

Atlantic Hotel

Le Mont de la Pulente, St Brelade; tel: 01534-744 101; www.theatlantichotel.com.

One of Jersey's most alluring hotels, with magnificent views over St Ouen's Bay and adjoining La Moye championship golf course. Gourmet cuisine is served in a lovely, light sea-view restaurant. Indoor and outdoor pools, health and leisure centre, all-weather tennis court. £££

Les Ormes Self Catering

Mont à la Brune, St Brelade's; tel: 01534-497 000; www.lesormesjersey.co.uk.

Contemporary and well-equipped self-catering resort comprising Les Ormes leisure village near St Brelade's Bay and Les Ormes de la Mer coastal cottages , overlooking St Ouen's Bay. Accommodation comes with well-equipped kitchens and pocket-sprung king-size beds. Les Ormes has a host of activities, including an indoor (and seasonal outdoor) pool, gym, indoor tennis, nine-hole golf course and fun zone; Les Ormes de la Mer has great surf and stunning sunsets (and the use of Les Ormes facilities). £744 −£1420 per apartment, per week.

L'Horizon Hotel & Spa

St Brelade's Bay; tel: 01534-743 101; www.handpickedhotels.co.uk/lhorizon

This luxurious and civilised beach hotel has a cool contemporary decor. Over half the 106 bedrooms have balconies overlooking the sea. There's a choice of restaurants, with alfresco dining in summer, plus a health club and spa with heated indoor pool. £££

St Brelade's Bay Hotel

St Brelade's Bay; tel: 01534-746 141; www.stbreladesbayhotel.com

Comfortable, relaxing hotel set in immaculate 7-acre (3-hectare) gardens and overlooking the best family beach on the island. Facilities include a state-of-the-art gym, health club and 20-metre swimming pool. £££

Windmills Hotel

Mont Gras d'Eau, St Brelade; tel: 01534-744 201; www.windmillshotel. com.

Long-established, family-run hotel set on the hillside, with fine views of St Brelade's and Ouaisné Bay. Spacious terrace gardens, outdoor heated pool, sauna and mini-gym. Self-catering apartments are also available. ££

Bouley Bay/Trinity/Rozel
Château La Chaire
Rozel Bay, St Martin; tel: 01534 863 354; www.chateau-la-chaire. co.uk

Traditional country house in a secluded spot near the sea at the foot of Rozel Valley. There are 14 luxury, individually-styled rooms, some with en suite spa bath and four-poster beds. The restaurant is noted for fine cuisine, and especially seafood. £££

Durrell Wildlife Camp

Les Augrès Manor, La Profonde Rue, Trinity; tel: 01534-860 090; www.dur rell.org/wildlife-park/luxury-camping

For something completely different experience the luxury camp at Jersey Zoo. Wake to the sound of lemurs or the sight of gibbons or red squirrels in the trees by your tent. Accommodation is comfy yurts with carpets, proper beds, wood-burning stoves and private bathrooms in separate tents. Cooking equipment is supplied and the zoo has two cafés. Guests have free access to the park and there are additional teepees for children if required. Minimum stay is normally three nights; seasonal. ££-£££

Fine dining at the Grand Jersey's Tassili restaurant.

Bask in the sunshine on the terrace of L'Horizon Hotel & Spa.

Undercliff Guest House

Bouley Bay, Trinity; tel: 0800-112 3058; www.undercliffjersey.com.

This is an ideal base for walkers, just 20 yards/metres from the spectacular north coast footpath. Bouley's pebble beach, with its clear waters, is down the road. Thirteen self-catering, individually styled en suite rooms as well as suites and two-bed apartments, garden with heated pool and friendly atmosphere. Bus to St Helier in season. £

Gorey
Beausite

Grouville Bay, Grouville; tel: 01534-857 577; www.beausite.com.

Near Grouville beach, the Beausite is a modern conversion of a 17th-century granite farm building and is very close to the Royal Jersey Golf Club. Child-friendly, with play area, games room and infants' pool as well as main pool. Self-catering apartments are also available. ££

St Saviour
Longueville Manor

St Saviour; tel: 01534-725 501; www.longuevillemanor.com.

The highest-rated hotel on the island, this elegant manor house is set in 15 acres (6 hectares) of gardens. The 14th-century building has been beautifully restored and is a member of the Relais & Châteaux group. The hotel is renowned for Jersey cuisine and has a heated outdoor pool and tennis court. £££

Websites

Visit Jersey (tel: 01534-859 000; www.jersey.com) has a free online booking service, whether for hotels, B&Bs, self-catering, camping or hostels.

Macole's (tel: 01534-488 100; www.macoles.com) offers a good choice of apartments and other self-catering accommodation.

Specialist Tour Operators:
www.airwaysholidays.com
www.citravelgroup.com
www.jerseytravel.com
www.condorbreaks.com (by ferry only)

Index

Accommodation 122

Battle of Flowers 57, 59
Battle of Jersey 21
beaches and swimming 112
Beauport 44
black butter 13
Black Dog of Bouley Bay 56
Bonne Nuit 71
Bouley Bay 69
buses 116

Car hire 117
Catherine's Ba 92
customs allowances 121
cycling 109, 118

Devil's Hole 74
disabled travellers 119
diving 112
driving 117
Durrell, Gerard 100
Durrell Wildlife Conservation Trust 101

Emergencies 119
entertainment 121
Eric Young Orchid Foundation 66

Facts for the visitor

119
ferries 118
fishing 111

Golf 113
Gorey 91
Green Island 95
Grève de Lecq 75
Grève de Lecq Barracks 76
Grosnez Castle 78

Hamptonne Country Life Museum 61
Höhlgangsanlage 8 32

Jersey bean crock 13
Jersey Lavender 64
Jersey War Tunnels 32

La Cotte de St Brelade 41
La Crête Fort 73
La Hougue Bie 85
La Mare Wine Estate 62
La Rocque 94
Le Dicq 98
Le Moulin de Lecq 76
Le Moulin de Tesson 64
Les Landes 77
L'Etacquerel 70
Lillie Langtry 82

Money 120

Mont Orgueil Castle 89
Moulin de Quétivel 63

Noirmont Point 39
north coast footpath 80

Opening times 120
Ouaisné Bay 40

Plémont 76
Portelet Bay 39

Ramsar Site 96
Royal Bay of Grouville 93
Rozel Bay 69

Sailing 111
Samarès Manor 96
sea kayaking/ coasteering 111
Seymour Tower 94
spas 114
St Aubin 36
St Aubin's Fort 38
St Brelade
   Church of St Brelade 43
   Fisherman's Chapel 43
St Brelade's Bay 41
St Helier
   Central Market 22
   Church of St Helier 18

Elizabeth Castle 25
Fish Market (Beresford Market) 23
Jersey Museum and Art Gallery 24
Liberation Sculpture 15
Liberation Square 15
Maritime Museum 16
New North Quay 16
Occupation Tapestry Gallery 18
Royal Court 22
Royal Square 20
Steam Clock 16
Waterfront 29
St Peter's Valley 63
surfing 110

Tamba Park 62
taxis 119
telephones 120
tourist information 121
travel documents 121

Walking 108
Waterworks Valley 60

Credits

Insight Guides Great Breaks Jersey
Editor: Tatiana Wilde
Author: Susie Bolton
Head of DTP and Pre-Press: Rebeka Davies
Picture Editor: Tom Smyth
Cartography Update: Carte
Photo credits: Alamy 113T; Alex Cordiner
56TL, 56/57T; Condor Ferries Ltd 115;
Corbis 82TL, 82ML, 82/83T; Dreamstime
90B; Fish 'n' Beads 42; Getty Images 27B,
42/43T, 72T, 73T, 98T, 106/107; Hand Picked
Hotels 125, 126; iStock 1, 4/5, 6ML, 12B,
51B, 72B, 74T, 80T; Leonardo 124; Mockford
& Bonetti/Apa Publications 6ML, 6MC, 6MC,
7T, 7M, 7TR, 7MR, 7BR, 7M, 8/9, 9, 11, 12T,
13, 14, 15T, 15B, 16, 17, 18/19T, 20T, 20B,
21, 22, 23B, 23T, 24T, 24B, 25, 26, 27T, 28B,
29T, 29B, 30B, 30T, 32TL, 32ML, 32/33T, 34,
35, 36, 37T, 37B, 38, 39T, 40B, 40T, 41T, 41B,
43B, 44T, 44B, 46, 48T, 48B, 49T, 49B, 50B,
50T, 51T, 52B, 52T, 53T, 53B, 54, 55, 56ML,
58, 59, 60B, 60T, 61T, 63B, 64T, 65, 66, 67,
68, 69T, 69B, 70, 71, 73B, 74B, 75B, 75T,
76B, 76T, 77, 78B, 78T, 79B, 80B, 81, 84, 86T,
86B, 87B, 87T, 88T, 88B, 89T, 89B, 90T, 91B,
91T, 92, 93T, 93B, 94T, 94B, 95T, 96T, 96B,
97T, 97B, 100B, 100T, 101, 102T, 103B, 103T,
104, 105T, 105B, 108, 109B, 109T, 110, 111T,
111B, 112T, 112B, 113B, 116, 117T, 117B,
118B, 118T, 119, 120B, 120T, 121; National
Trust for Jersey 64B; Penguin Books 102B;
Public domain 18B, 19, 28T, 39B, 95B, 98B;
Ralph on flickr 79T; Shutterstock 10; Tamba
Park 62, 63T; The Club Hotel & Spa 114,
123; The Jersey Club 122; The Pallot Steam,
Motor & General Museum 61B
Cover credits: Reinhard Schmid/4Corners
Images (main) Mockford & Bonetti/Apa
Publications (bottom L&R)

Distribution
UK, Ireland and Europe: Apa Publications
(UK) Ltd; sales@insightguides.com
United States and Canada: Ingram Publisher
Services; ips@ingramcontent.com
Australia and New Zealand: Woodslane;
info@woodslane.com.au
Southeast Asia: Apa Publications (SN) Pte;
singaporeoffice@insightguides.com
Worldwide: Apa Publications (UK) Ltd;
sales@insightguides.com
**Special Sales, Content Licensing and
CoPublishing**
Insight Guides can be purchased in bulk
quantities at discounted prices. We can
create special editions, personalised
jackets and corporate imprints tailored
to your needs. sales@insightguides.com;
www.insightguides.biz